Living Holiness

Living Holiness

Stanley Hauerwas and the Church

John B. Thomson

scm press

Published in 2012 by SCM Press
Editorial office
3rd Floor, Invicta House
108–114 Golden Lane
London EC1Y 0TG

Previously published in 2010 by
Epworth Press
Methodist Church House
25 Marylebone Road
London NW1 5JR

SCM Press is an imprint of Hymns Ancient & Modern Ltd
(a registered charity)
13A Hellesdon Park Road
Norwich NR6 5DR, UK

www.scmpress.co.uk

British Library Cataloguing in Publication data

A catalogue record for this book is available
from the British Library

978-0-334-04604-2
Kindle 978-0-334-04605-9

Typeset by Regent Typesetting, London
Printed and bound in Great Britain by
CPI Group (UK) Ltd, Croydon CR0 4YY

Contents

Preface and Acknowledgements

Stanley Hauerwas was described in *Time* magazine (2001) as 'America's best theologian',[1] and he remains one of the most creative Christian thinkers in the North Atlantic context. As a church minister in both congregational and diocesan settings I have found his insights creative, refreshing and very challenging, particularly in the following areas:

- *The Church:* why belonging to the Church is vital for Christian discipleship today as a witness to the Kingdom of God.
- *Worship:* how worship transforms Christians into witnesses of the gospel.
- *Ethics:* the distinctive virtues and contextual character of Christian discipleship as living holiness.
- *Practices:* how the social activities and habits of the Church are vital to discipleship development and witness.
- *Character:* who we are as Christian communities informs how we live out and witness to our faith.
- *Truth:* how truthfulness, tragedy and suffering belong together.
- *Story:* the remarkable character of the Christian story which we are invited to inhabit and within which our own discipleship stories are given meaning.
- *Scripture:* how we need to be formed into a holy people if we are to interpret the Scriptures truthfully. Individualistic reading corrupts Scripture.
- *Virtue:* what is distinctive about Christian virtues and the impact they have on our living.
- *Politics:* why the theological politics of the Church, its communal

way of living together with God, matters so much as a witness to the world.

- *Friendship:* what sharing in the hospitable friendship of Jesus implies for disciples today.
- *Freedom:* how true freedom involves embracing God's way together rather than seeking to be autonomous.
- *Peace:* that the distinctive character of the Church is robust peaceableness in a violent world.
- *Faith:* that faith is a trusting way of communal living with Christ rather than a package of ideas and that faithfulness is what characterizes discipleship rather than ambiguous notions of success, effectiveness or statistical impact.
- *Language:* the way Christians should live is like a language which describes how God loves the world.
- *Suffering:* living within the story of God's love for the world gives Christians a distinctive way of interpreting suffering and tragedy.

In short, Stanley Hauerwas directs us to the resources God has graced us with to witness to the world that it is loved, cherished and sought by God its Creator and Redeemer. He shows us what it means to be a Christian community today in very tangible terms. He helps to restore confidence in the Christian project at a time when it is being severely challenged. He has a lot to offer the Church, and I have felt for some time that an accessible and relatively short introduction, together with improvisations explored at ground-level ministry, would be helpful. In offering this book, I am attempting to fill this gap.

Part One is therefore an introduction to Hauerwas and his work. In these chapters I look at how he flags up the importance of the Church, its story and its communal life, as witness to the reign of God in the world. I also discuss aspects of this thought which are particularly contentious:

- In Chapter 1, 'Recovering Holiness', I expound the main contours of his work on character, virtue and the Church in late modern societies and why it developed in this way.

- In Chapter 2, 'Narrating Holiness', I look more closely at the importance of narrative and story in his work as a resource for the church's mission.
- In Chapter 3, 'Embodying Holiness', I explore what Hauerwas understands by the distinctive politics of the Church and why it is so important for its mission.
- In Chapter 4, 'Challenging Holiness', I discuss some of the significant challenges levelled at him and try to respond to these as a critical friend.

In Part Two I try to improvise on discipleship, ministry and mission themes which Hauerwas's work helped me to see in a new light.

- In Chapter 5, 'Congregational Holiness', I show how his work sheds light on the mission of an ordinary congregation.
- In Chapter 6, 'Sharing Holiness', I show how I developed a discipleship course using insights from his thinking.
- In Chapter 7, 'Discerning Holiness', I explore the way his work impacts on Scripture.
- In Chapter 8, 'Cultivating Holiness', I discuss the impact of his views upon mission.
- In Chapter 9, 'Witnessing Holiness', I look at his distinctive apologetics.
- In Chapter 10, 'Living Holiness', I try to show how Hauerwas helps us to witness confidently with some of the major challenges confronting Christians in late modern societies.

Holy people have halos. They exude light. They exude God. There are numerous people whose halos have helped me to understand what living holiness means. I am grateful to the congregations of St Mary's, Wheatley, and St Peter's, Warmsworth, both in Doncaster, England, whose bread-and-butter holiness has so enriched and challenged me over the past 15 years. I am grateful to the Africans of my Uganda childhood and of my time in South Africa, whose robust and lively holiness impressed upon me the serious yet joyful character of Christian living and the significance of common worship. I am grateful to my mother and late father for embodying adventurous holiness in their calling to serve in Uganda. I am grateful to my wife Sue and daughters Anya and Emily, whose patience with the poverty of my own holiness helps me to experience the lively grace of God. In addition, particular thanks go to Stanley Hauerwas for helping me to see more clearly what it means to be holy today, and to the Dioceses of Argentina and Newcastle, Australia, who offered me hospitality and the opportunity to test out some of the material in this book during visits in 2005 and 2006. Thanks also go to Graham Pigott, my spiritual director, who patiently keeps before me the challenge of living holiness; to James Bond, Malcolm Fair, Amanda Fair, Mark James, Therese Paskell, Martyn Percy and Vernon White for reading initial drafts and making helpful suggestions; to Angela Shier-Jones of Epworth Press for her incisive and pertinent editorial suggestions; and to my colleagues in the Ministry and Mission Department of the Diocese of Sheffield who often wonder, I am sure, what on earth I am scribbling next. We never walk alone.

Note

1 *Time* magazine, 17 September 2001.

Part One

Introducing Stanley Hauerwas

1

Recovering Holiness[1]

My interest in Stanley Hauerwas emerged while I was a church minister in inner-urban Doncaster struggling to discern the vocation of a Christian community in the traditionally low churchgoing area of south Yorkshire in England. In addition it was evoked by limitations in my understanding of the place of the Church in discipleship and witness and by the influence of liberation and other theologies which I had encountered while a theological educator in South Africa. Hauerwas helped me to see living holiness as the Church's witness in western societies and also as the condition for a deeper understanding of God's action in the world.

Such an understanding of living holiness does not require a deceptively romantic view of the Church. Rather it suggests that as Christians practise faith in company with other Christian pilgrims, past and present, they find themselves being formed into a particular sort of people. God's grace does something to their identities which speaks of God's own character and disposition. In short, discipleship is living holiness which, for Hauerwas, expresses itself in peaceableness and friendship. This does not mean that he provides a blueprint for the Church or an idealistic vision of that Church's calling. Instead, he shows us that attention to the conditions and dispositions appropriate to living holiness will enable Christians to discover the call of God in contemporary life. Practising faith therefore forms Christians to see the journey of faith as a way of life that is not a human-centred activity but a co-operation with the action of God in worship and mission. Consequently Hauerwas believes the principal agent in the witness of the Church to be God, and living holiness is primarily the holiness of God transforming the Church into faithful witnesses to God's reign. Hence in this chapter I introduce some key themes from his work. In Chapters 2 and 3 I will look at the way his reflections on the Church's story and its politics illuminate this way of holiness. In Chapter 4 I will discuss some of the challenges that his work has evoked.

Stanley Hauerwas

Stanley Hauerwas was born on 24 July 1940 in Pleasant Grove, Texas. The son of a gentle Texan bricklayer and tenacious, vocal Mississippi mother, he was raised as a Methodist within the Revivalist tradition and educated in local schools. Thereafter his intellectual gifts enabled him to study philosophy at Southwestern University in Texas and then theology at Yale Divinity School where his main interest was in Christian ethics and where he wrote his doctorate.[2] He then became a theological educator, teaching first in the Lutheran Augustana College and then at the Roman Catholic University of Notre Dame. His present post at the Methodist Duke University in Durham, North Carolina, is Gilbert Ryle Professor of Theological Ethics. During the past 35 years, Hauerwas has written over 300 essays and many sermons, and these, together with his diverse pedigree, make him very difficult to typify. He describes himself a Methodist who is a 'Mennonite camp follower'.[3]

Holy ethics

Hauerwas's initial aim in the 1970s was to recover resources for a distinctively Christian ethic, or way of life, which he believed had been corroded by the legacy of post-Enlightenment liberalism. The eighteenth-century Enlightenment was a North Atlantic movement of thought that distrusted tradition and authorities in all matters of intellectual enquiry and believed that truth could only be obtained through reason, observation and experiment. In consequence the quest for secure knowledge became a human-centred activity with the aim of liberating human exploration from its perceived theological shackles and the bloody conflicts these shackles had imposed upon Europe in the seventeenth-century wars of religion. This way of thinking is associated with René Descartes and Immanuel Kant. Descartes sought to find security by doubting everything until he could 'discover one thing only which is certain and indubitable'.[4] This he claimed to find in the phrase '*cogito ergo sum*' ('I think therefore I exist'), which he believed freed him from tyrannies such as tradition and prejudice. Kant developed this foundationalism further by positing the transcendental subject as the autonomous unit for human understanding and knowledge. This subject was stripped of all particulars which distinguished it from other subjects, thereby enabling generalizations about human identity and knowing to be made. From this Cartesianism emerged a form of positivism deemed to be compatible with the increasingly impressive methodology of the natural sciences. Human beings could survey the universe confident in the security of their capacities as knowing creatures and sure that their senses offered them a truthful account of the world those senses engaged with. This knowledge appeared much more robust than theological claims to truth and reversed the order of knowing by beginning with human consciousness and sensory perception rather than divine revelation.

However, Hauerwas believes that the problem with such thinking is that it misguidedly and simplistically assumes an abstract and universally valid spectator approach to discovering the truth about reality. We do not need to be formed into people who can understand or recognize what is true. Nor do we need to pay attention to the communities and contexts which contribute to this formation and which situate all truth claims. In this he stands within a tradition critical of such Enlightenment universalism. For example, the nineteenth-century philosopher Hegel was among the first to recognize the effect of historical consciousness upon human ways of understanding. He noted the significance of the particular and the historical and social shaping of human structures of consciousness. Schleiermacher and then Dilthey continued to explore the notion of historical consciousness and the way understanding human beings differed from the knowledge sought by the natural sciences. Inter-subjectivity, linguistic awareness and interpretative skills were required rather than simply observation and measurement. Later, the 'masters of suspicion' – Marx, Freud and Nietzsche – raised questions about the innocence of human consciousness, questioning how far subjects were in possession of their identity, while the philosopher Heidegger stressed the situatedness of the human subject and the limitations this placed on human understanding. Ironically this opened the way for Hans-Georg Gadamer and Alasdair MacIntyre to rehabilitate tradition and prejudice as the contexts within which human knowing gains its intelligibility, since to be situated is to be within an existing world and language. Other, more radical thinkers such as Lyotard, Derrida, Foucault and Rorty, stressed the situatedness of the subject in time, thereby rendering it fluid and unstable and its claims to truthful insight merely aspirations to power. Jürgen Habermas, on the other hand, tried to recover the critical possibilities of human understanding by accepting the inter-subjective character of knowing and seeking for approximations to the ideal speech situation in an open and inclusive conversational community.[5]

Hauerwas's work is part of a wider debate about the legacy of the Enlightenment. He, along with others, challenges the Enlightenment's confidence in the singular and abstract subject able to grasp the meaning of the world as a sort of spectator. The thinking subject is always embedded in contexts and communities which both dispose and form that subject to interpret the world and human living within it in ways related to that embeddedness. Consequently, since there is no neutrality in human thought, Hauerwas argues that Christians ought to articulate their own distinctive vision of human living without embarrassment in public discussion. They should not be reduced to silence by a self-deceptively confident way of thinking rooted in a false notion of spectator objectivity.

To do this, Christians will need to re-engage with the themes of sanctification, character and practical reason as resources for displaying a distinctively Christian way of life.[6] Sanctification describes the timeful display of God's holiness in human lives. It enables the shape of Christian discipleship to be traced and recognized and allows for the form of Christian living to be displayed, particularly by those the Church calls saints. This form of living is what Hauerwas calls character. Character, he believes, is about human identity, which is formed as people participate in particular stories and communities. It is not about being a character in the popular sense of the term but is about having character, a moral history, which indicates a person's true identity and disposes them to make choices faithful to their identity. Practical reason is the wisdom for negotiating the challenges of life in the light of one's character and its co-relative history. It involves being trained to make good judgements and choices in an ever-changing world informed by one's character and the story of life generative of that character. To be so rooted in a formative story also implies actively participating in the life of the community whose story this is. For Christians, this community is the Church, through which they discover and witness to truthful knowledge about God and the human situation.

Such an approach leads Hauerwas to explore the nature of human formation, sight, training and virtue.[7] Influenced by Iris Murdoch and her attempt to attend to and see the good truthfully, he argues that Christians need to be formed and trained to see life and its challenges in a way analogous to 'an artist engaged in his work rather than a critic making a judgment about a finished product'.[8] Since no one is an abstract spectator, such training involves inhabiting and employing the wisdom of the Christian community. Such communal wisdom provides a distinctively Christian way of 'seeing' or describing issues such as abortion, the care of children and the elderly, euthanasia and disability. For example, Christians believe that a good death (euthanasia) is one that leaves a good memory and trustfully locates that death in the ongoing story of the grace of God embodied in the Church. In liberal ethics, autonomy disconnects people from this communal story, subverts any sense of history and undermines the capacity of a community to celebrate the lives of the elderly by caring for them. Furthermore, caring for children, the disabled and the elderly reflects the Christian commitment to welcome the new and strange which self-centred liberal ethics finds increasingly conflictual with its autonomous convictions. Thus Hauerwas is distinguishing Christian ethics from liberal ethics by showing that the former flow from the character of its story and community life. As a result he believes that there will be diverse ethical views in any society, and consequently Christians must not be silent about articulating their distinctive way of life.

Yet in the light of such ethical pluralism, how can Hauerwas claim that Christian ethics be truthful wisdom? In addition, how can his approach avoid promoting an anarchic and confusing ethical relativism which cannot resolve competing truth claims? The key is to pay attention to those experiences which human beings cannot will or choose, those experiences which impact upon them from beyond their consciousness and which cannot be contrived. Such experiences are truthful precisely because we would not choose them. They have an integrity which prevents self-deception. Two particular examples of this are the experience of tragedy and encountering something alien.[9] Tragedy and the challenge of the alien remind Christians that they do not control their destiny. Both impose themselves from without and force a response. In particular, tragedy breaks through any self-deception in a way which causes a response to a truth that cannot be denied or wished away. Furthermore, the tragic also indicates that humans are creatures in time, since tragedy profoundly changes them. Tragedy reveals the narrative shape of life. It is no accident, for Hauerwas, that the Christian way is expressed through narrative, and this leads him to explore the role of story in Christian formation, as we shall see below.[10]

Yet in order for this account of the tragic to be plausible, there needs to be a Church whose way of life situates such tragedy within a narrative of hope and expresses this hopeful story in the way it embraces such strange experiences in a hospitable manner. Such hospitality speaks of the Christian conviction that the stranger has a place in God's economy rather than being an enemy to be rejected. In drawing attention to such a practical response to tragedy,

Hauerwas roots the truthfulness of Christianity in the practices of Christian living rather than in ideological terms. These practices exhibit the story of God told by Israel and the Church, belong to the whole Church and are therefore less likely to be the vested interests of individuals or groups. The divine story is mediated by these practices and is rendered intelligible by the way they form the community's life.

Holy story

This relationship between story and Church in Christian ethics is developed most explicitly in Hauerwas's famous work *A Community of Character*.[11] For Hauerwas, Christian ethics are narrative ethics and are essentially social and political in character. They express the way the Christian community seeks to live and order its way of living within the ongoing story of God's grace. As a result they are parasitic upon the narrative of God's salvation disclosed by Christ and now embodied in the ordered life or polity of the Church. Thus the first responsibility of the Church is to become itself, since 'the truthfulness of Jesus creates and is known by the kind of community his story should form'.[12] Hauerwas argues that churches need to become more self-conscious of their particular identity as Christian communities before they engage in outreach to the world. Who Christians are takes priority over what Christians do, since what they do will flow from who they are. In addition, who Christians are is crucial to the witness of the Church, since, as the body of Christ and a people of hope, they are the witness which the world sees, judges and responds to.[13]

Such narrative ethics represent a conversation between the inherited story of faith remembered by the Church and the ongoing formation of the contemporary Church as it seeks to follow the way of Jesus. It is the story of the peaceable love of God in Christ crucified, and Christians seek to describe their living through this story. Consequently discipleship is determined by descriptions, since the story and its language give a distinctive purchase on reality and the Church's calling within this. In particular the focal plot of the story, the death and resurrection of Jesus, indicates that peaceableness is the interpretative key to the story of God witnessed to and lived by the Church. Consequently the truthfulness of the Gospel story is witnessed to by the practical and peaceable story of the Church rather than by metaphysical argument. Similarly the self is found through participating in this common narrative rather than in advance of it. The self is a traditioned and social identity in formation rather than the abstract, individualistic and fixed autonomous entity of liberal thought or the anarchic fluidity of postmodernity. Located in space and time, Hauerwas believes that the self is created as it inhabits and is trained by the story of God's grace and finds the particulars of its own story integrated and stabilized within this great epic. Part of the test of the truthfulness of this story and its peaceableness is its capacity to embrace those, like Hauerwas's Uncle Charlie, an Alzheimer sufferer, who is no longer an autonomous human agent and whose identity can only be given by a story which integrates him within the community of God's universal grace.[14]

Holy politics

A particular consequence of this narrative identity is that the Church rather than society or the state is the primary community for Christians. Christian loyalty is to God before any human organization, and Christians are to live in a manner relevant to the agenda of God rather than to the agenda of those with power or influence in the world. Such relevance to God's agenda mediated through worship, Scripture and the history of discipleship, equips the Church to discern how to witness to the grace of God in diverse contexts. In particular, such loyalty enables Christians to discern when the state is demanding too much from them. This is in contrast to Constantinianism, which Hauerwas regards as the control of the Church by the state consequent upon the emperor Constantine's conversion in the fourth century and which he feels continues in various guises today. While Constantinianism remains the public religious settlement in Europe, Hauerwas is particularly worried about its hidden character within American democracy. He believes that this form of political order has been uncritically embraced by most American Christians without realizing that its roots lie in a liberal understanding of human identity. It has had the effect of diminishing the political significance of the Church in American Christianity, particularly its Protestant expression. As a result, many American Christians believe that they can be disciples without participating in the sort of training and formation Hauerwas advocates and can read the Scriptures without being inducted into the traditions of scriptural reading that have shaped the Church's appropriation of those Scriptures. Indeed, to many Americans words such as 'autonomy', 'democracy', 'freedom' and 'choice' as well as a phrases such as 'the freedom of religion' are part of Christian vocabulary. In effect he believes that this represents liberal thinking colonizing American Christians and co-opting them to its cause. This is a hidden form of Constantinianism since it ensures that Christians are citizens before they are disciples and are more likely to follow the demands of the state without question than challenge the state on the basis of their primary loyalty to the Church. One of these demands is to take part in the state's wars, and it is this demand which Hauerwas believes lies at the heart of the contest between Constantinianism and faithful discipleship.

In contrast, Hauerwas believes that the truthfulness of the gospel is displayed first in the capacity of the Church as Christ's body to embrace difference peaceably through Christlike embrace of the stranger, second by facing the tragic with hope reflective of Jesus embracing the cross, and third by attracting people to faith from all communities. Peaceableness, therefore, characterizes Hauerwas's understanding of the Church, or his ecclesiology.[15] Peaceable living is the Church's primary witness to God's peaceable victory achieved in Christ, since the risen and ascended Christ reigns in the present. Consequently the Church is not responsible for transforming the world into the Kingdom of God, since the Kingdom is already present in the world. Instead, its calling is to witness through its life of holiness to the presence of the reigning Christ in its midst. In this he distinguishes himself from two of North

America's significant Protestant traditions: the social gospel of Walter Rauschenbusch and the responsible realism of Reinhold Niebuhr. Rauschenbusch is associated with the social gospel movement of the late nineteenth century, which regarded the Church as a prophetic vanguard movement whose agenda was to transform society into the Kingdom of God in partnership with socialist and progressivist politics. It was love in action, a reaction against contemporary Protestant pietism, and it was optimistic about the possibilities for a symphonic relationship between Church and state. Reinhold Niebuhr's responsible realism was a reaction against the optimism and naivety of the social gospel movement, particularly with regard to the effects of sin upon individuals and collectives. Niebuhr was more sceptical about the capacity of the gospel story to transform society, and instead regarded the ministry of Jesus as an impossible ideal whose purpose was to relativize all human social projects and subvert utopias. All that Christians could do was to approximate to this ideal within the finitude and fallenness of life, a form of relative pragmatism where the best was always the best possible rather than the absolute ideal. Human politics was the art of the possible informed by the myths of the Christian story, such as the Fall, yet not seeking to represent an embodiment of the reign of God.

Although the social gospel and responsible realism movements appeared contradictory, both, for Hauerwas, proffered ethics which, in seeking to redeem the world by human effort, simply underwrote the liberal order with its confidence in human agency and practical atheism. They thereby rendered the Church redundant as a divinely infused life-transforming community. Rauschenbusch's Church let its agenda be set by progressivist interpretations of society rooted in the sort of optimistic and imperialistic liberal assumptions that denied the intrinsic necessity of the Church and its story for truthful politics. As such, the Church was simply a reservoir for activists and the Kingdom of God merely a series of ideas to be realized by human agency rather than the existing reign of God to which the politics of the Church bears witness.[16] Niebuhr's project effectively gave legitimacy to violence, since, by relegating Jesus to a transcendent but irrelevant ideal, it left the real political decisions to the perspective and interests of those with coercive power. For Niebuhr, all that the Church could achieve was an approximation to the ideal of Jesus' witness because he believed it had to be realistic about the fallen condition of human societies and individuals. The Church cannot embody the peaceableness of Christ, with the result that violence is sometimes a tragic but necessary action as the lesser of two evils. According to Niebuhr, Jesus' Kingdom in its fullness is yet to come and belongs to the Second Advent era. Contemporary politics is a pragmatic affair seeking to do what is possible within a series of competing ambiguous demands.

In contrast, Hauerwas believes that Christians are called to witness that Jesus' peaceable reign is already present and needs no force to establish or maintain it.[17] The fullness of Jesus' life is present in his Church and there is nothing that the Second Advent will disclose which is not already present in the world. Christians can therefore live peaceably and offer space and time to the 'small' things of life, such as having children or visiting the sick, since in so doing they display their confidence that God reigns.[18] This is the exhibition of their confidence that God rather than humankind controls the world's destiny. Hauerwas is therefore arguing for a different understanding of history which is informed by his mentor, John Howard Yoder. This view sees history as redeemed and infused by the eschatological effects of Christ's peaceable ministry, death and resurrection. The reign of God is present and focused, though not exhausted, by the Church. Christians therefore live within this reality rather than within the histories assumed by either the social gospel movement or Niebuhr's responsible realism. These approaches presume that God's reign is yet to be completed and that human agency is critical either to bring it about or to manage a fallen world until that Kingdom comes in its fullness.[19]

As a consequence of this historiography Hauerwas believes the just-war theory to be a form of compromised Christian practice since it represents concerns for control, relevance and violence in contrast to living Christ's peaceableness. The just-war theory was developed by Augustine of Hippo and subsequent thinkers in order to limit the violence of war by providing a series of criteria which established whether a war was just or not. It was premised on the impossibility of absolute pacifism. Following John Howard Yoder, Hauerwas holds that its eschatology, or grasp of God's destiny for creation, is deficient since it sidesteps the significance for the Church's witness of Jesus' peaceable ministry. Furthermore, the just-war theory fails to expose the fundamental coalition between violence, war and the liberal state despite the latter's democratic rhetoric. Without any other resources for social cohesion, Hauerwas argues that war becomes essential for liberal states which are effectively a coalition of individuals. In contrast he believes that the Church is God's word about war since it is configured to peaceableness.[20] By living peaceably it speaks a message about God's ways with the world which is about a true cruciform and peaceable power that unmasks the hubris of those violent powers that seek to rule illegitimately and destructively.[21] Among other things, the peaceable Church provides space for trust, friendship, having children, welcoming the outsider and reconciliation. In addition it embodies a counter-narrative to the corrosive effects of global capitalism by rejecting the privatization of everything and the consequent loss of any sense of memory and tradition.[22] The Church also possesses resources for ecological respect since its story speaks of a creator and a creation rather than a human preoccupied community exploiting 'nature' for its own ends.[23]

Holy performance

As Hauerwas's work develops, increasingly he gives primacy to the performance of Christian living rather than simply to the rhetoric of Christian belief.[24] As we have seen, he argues that since there is no universal, spectator or objective view of human ethics, ethical languages are parasitic upon the traditions of existing communities and their practices which, in Christian terms, means the Church. The Church is God's new language and describes the Christian way by its manner of life.[25] This language, for example, flags up the theological significance of mundane Christian practices such as building a church in an inner urban area or providing an open Sunday meal to the homeless as an extension of the Eucharist.[26] These performances exemplify the way Christians believe God acts in the world. Furthermore, they remind us that, in order to understand the Church and its calling, we must pay attention to the stories and practices of particular churches such as Broadway and Aldersgate Methodist Churches which Hauerwas himself attended. In such tangible communities Christians learn how to live as disciples and through corporate worship are formed to see their contextual Christian vocation in the world.[27] This living holiness shapes the vision of the Church so that as Christians perform their story they discover a liberty that enables them to serve the world on God's terms and, in peaceable living, to witness to the truthfulness of the Christian gospel.[28]

Such performances function as a language describing God's ways with the world and, as God's new language, the Church 'speaks' in various dialects since, although the Church's primary identity is Christian, among its members are people with secondary but significant identities, such as race, gender or nationality. Hauerwas himself is a Christian who is also a Texan.[29] In addition he is convinced that the truth of Christianity is witnessed to primarily in the way the Church lives rather than in abstract debates about the status of its Scripture, since speaking a language is fundamentally a performance rather than simply rhetoric. Indeed, the Scriptures are insufficient without the Church and cannot be properly understood without the Church since the Church represents both the interpretative key and embodied expression of the divine narrative born witness to by these texts. Ecclesial training through participating in the formative life of the Church is essential if a proper interpretation of the Scriptures is to be had.[30] For the Christian to read the Bible on one's own and untrained is an exercise in misunderstanding it since the Bible will not be functioning as the Christian community's Scriptures, but rather as a series of abstract ancient texts disconnected from the community whose contemporary and historical life identifies them as its Scriptures.[31]

Holy freedom

Hauerwas's project is about recovering holy freedom which he believes the Church has lost in its alliance with patterns of thought rooted in the Enlightenment. These patterns are often called liberalism and reflect a quest for the freedom of the individual from the constraints of religion, history and society in favour of a way of life which privileges autonomy and the present moment. This form of liberalism strips human identity of its particularities, its narrative character and its intrinsically social nature as it seeks to promote an anthropology based upon an abstract self voluntarily relating to others on the basis of self-interest. Such an anthropology has no understanding of formation and of the virtues, and approaches ethics in an instrumental and calculative manner. Happiness is the goal for the liberal autonomous self and so decisions are made in a utilitarian and consequentialist manner. Yet this fails to recognize that human beings are embedded within the world rather than spectators of it. They are creatures of space and time who become who they are through participating in narrative communities rather than remaining autonomous agents whose decisions are unaffected by such contexts. Liberal ethics seeks to divorce means from ends which Hauerwas regards as impossible since the means are in the ends. Who we become informs how we see the ends and what those ends become. For Christians, the virtues shape our vision and enable us to see what ends are appropriate for disciples. When Christians forget who they are and seek to be relevant to the liberal agenda, they are colonized by this agenda and the Church becomes irrelevant and is subverted.

The best analogy Hauerwas offers for the corrupting and colonizing character of liberalism is contemporary medicine.[32] Liberalism subverts medicine as technology and autonomous individualism conspire to promote an instrumental, abstract and utilitarian approach to curing people. This loses touch with the traditional practices, wisdom and caring vocation of medicine. The liberal doctor is now a health technician whose technical approach to medicine reduces patients to units of disease. The particulars of the patients and their distinctive stories are less important than their character as examples of disease needing curing. Consequently medicine ironically loses touch with the body and becomes increasingly about abstractions. It becomes docetic and disembodied. Yet at the same time doctors become state bureaucrats offering non-directional choices to autonomous patients who must choose their own medical care. This undermines the doctors' role as medical authorities since the authority for medical treatment is abdicated to the autonomous patient. In addition, technology has caused medicine to be idolized and has contributed to the idea that medicine can eliminate sickness and ensure a healthy norm in society, often by eliminating the sick in the name of ridding the world of sickness. Such medicine easily becomes tyrannical and hostile to the abnormal given its conviction that suffering is always bad and to be got rid of. Its theodicy represents a form of human hubris as it presumes that there is a singular problem called suffering which can be identified by a spectator grasp of reality. This challenges traditional Christian understandings of God's ways with the world and asserts that human agency alone can respond adequately to this problem.

Hauerwas sees in the corruption of medicine an analogy with the corruption of the Church by liberal thinking. The stress upon autonomy, the absence of an explicit narrative identity, the focus upon abstractions which can be relocated across time and space, the reduction of human beings to abstract types, the stress upon efficiency and calculus, the loss of a sense of tradition, a misplaced confidence in the ethical agent as spectator rather than artist, the displacement of virtues in favour of rules and usefulness, and the loss of any sense of community have a combined acidic effect upon the Church. Christians infected with this philosophy come to believe that they can dispense with the Church or treat is as another voluntary collective which is not a necessary contributor to their discipleship. They lose the sense of the Church as a school of virtue apprenticed to the saints whose vocation is to witness, corporeally and peaceably, to the present reign of God as it inhabits the story of God's salvation. They doubt the value of suffering since it is no longer seen as an interpretation of diverse painful experiences within God's hopeful story.

In this critique of contemporary liberalism within North Atlantic societies, Hauerwas finds allies in the likes of theologians Karl Barth, Hans Frei and George Lindbeck. Barth remains the arch-critic of the German liberal tradition which he regarded as capitulating to World War One and colluding with the rise of Nazism in World War Two because it had allowed theology to become anthropology and let consciousness replace the Church as the environment for revelation. In its place Barth advocated dogmatics as a theology of contingent response or *Nachdenken*, to the free self-disclosure of the divine in Jesus Christ. Such a response was necessarily narrative as it traced the Church's response to God's revelation in Christ the Word mediated through the stories of Scripture. It was also a theology which began with God's self-disclosure rather than with human experience or consciousness, thereby attempting to escape from the reduction of God to human categories of thought. In Barth's thinking, the Church acts as herald to this revelation and its ethics involve a moment-by-moment obedience to the contemporary word of God. As a result Barth, like Hauerwas, rejects any apologetics which seeks to frame theology within the categories of liberal thinking.

Hans Frei and George Lindbeck similarly seek to rescue the Christian story from captivity to liberal thought.[33] Frei seeks to do this by taking further Barth's emphasis upon story and narrative and arguing that the truthfulness of the scriptural story is discovered as the self is enfolded into its narrative whose plausibility is underscored by the historic existence of a Church which calls these stories Scripture. Lindbeck challenges the notion that liberal thinking rests upon secure foundations and instead argues that different religions represent distinctive languages which seek to make sense of the world. They cannot be reduced to one universally agreed view of reality since no one is a spectator of life. Instead, people find themselves in one or other of these languages and test out their plausibility by living through them.

Hauerwas's sympathies for these theological critiques of liberalism do not mean that he uncritically espouses them. As we have argued, Hauerwas is convinced that the Church is the focal environment for Christian narrative ethics. He is therefore critical of Barth's preoccupation with the texts of Scripture at the expense of the politics of the Church. God's word is in the Church rather than beyond it, and the story of God is held in the community rather than existing alongside it. Bodies have priority over texts and embodiment is the critical witness rather than literary cohesion. As he says, 'I try to do theology in a manner that exposes the politics and material conditions of Christian speech.'[34] Equally he is committed to the tangible persuasiveness of the Church's witness rather than the rhetorical persuasiveness of dogmatics. Thus 'we follow Jesus before we know him'.[35] For Hauerwas it is the community of the Church which brings the Scriptures to life, whereas for Barth it is the Scriptures which bring the Church to life. This means that sanctification as a tangible and ongoing transformation of the Church is crucial for the latter's witness in a way that Barth has reservations about. Similarly, he is concerned that Frei and Lindbeck miss the vital role of the Church in rendering the faith plausible. 'All theology must begin and end with ecclesiology', since texts are silent without practices and people.[36] The Church, therefore, is the language which is spoken in its faithful practices, rather than the language being addressed to the Church as the premise for its transformation. Jesus is therefore known in the life of his disciples.

In criticizing liberalism, Hauerwas is not rejecting its insights out of hand. He writes, 'My problem has never been with secular political liberals but rather with the widespread assumption shared by many Christians, that political liberalism ought to shape the agenda, if not the way of life, of the Church.'[37] Liberalism is a distinctive tradition which emerged in reaction to the Christian tradition but is not a way of thinking to which Christians must default. As he comments when rejecting the notion that Christians should withdraw from the service of their neighbours, 'The object of my criticism has never been liberals, but rather to give Christians renewed confidence in the convictions that make our service intelligible.'[38] Christians should engage with liberals as Christians who can discern what of liberalism is compatible with Christian practice. They do not capitulate to its claims to be a neutral and universal language about reality. Indeed, Hauerwas believes that Christians have serious problems with liberalism since it is the theoretical expression of a destructive capitalism that seeks to reduce all to consumers who produce nothing and has no sense of time within which human beings can discover their identity and relationships. His work represents an attempt to deconstruct the pretentions of this liberalism and to offer a more substantial way of living through the Church. Hence he challenges liberalism's universalist claims, its equation of freedom with autonomy, its notion of politics as the procedural balancing of interest groups, its loss of any sense of the common good, its privatizing of religion and its dependency on war for social cohesion.[39] In its place he simply offers the Church.

Conclusion

Hauerwas reminds the Church that its core witness is living holiness, the tangible and communal expression of faith in flesh. As such, the Church is an embodied apologetic, a tangible witness that gives a rationale for God's saving action in the world and an expression of the wisdom of God in creation.[40] Indeed, the presence of holy Christian communities formed by the practices of worship and discipleship to discern and share in God's mission in the world offers a creative and contextually embodied witness for the present time. This chapter has explored how Hauerwas recovers the pivotal role of the Church in God's mission as a community with a distinctively Christian ethic, story, politics, performance and freedom. In the next two chapters I want to look more closely at the way his reflections on the story and politics of the Church indicate to contemporary Christians what it means to be a community living holiness.

Questions

- What new insights have you gained from Hauerwas's understanding of the Church?
- What do you make of his focus upon character, peaceableness and performance as crucial for Christian witness?
- How might Hauerwas's approach to the Church change your church?
- Can you connect Hauerwas's project with his Methodist roots?
- Can you begin to formulate any criticisms of his project?

Further reading

Hauerwas, Stanley, *A Community of Character: Toward a Constructive Christian Social Ethic*, 4th edn, Notre Dame: University of Notre Dame Press, 1986.

—— *The Peaceable Kingdom: A Primer in Christian Ethics*, 3rd edn, Notre Dame and London: University of Notre Dame Press, 1986.

Hauerwas, Stanley and William H. Willimon, *Where Resident Aliens Live: Exercises for Christian Practices*, Nashville: Abingdon Press, 1996.

Notes

1 This chapter is based on a paper first published as 'Stanley Hauerwas and Christian Community', in *The Epworth Review*, 32.1, 2005, pp. 37–46. My thanks to the Revd Canon Professor Martyn Percy for his comments on the initial drafts. For an exploration of Hauerwas's project see John B. Thomson, *The Ecclesiology of Stanley Hauerwas: A Christian Theology of Liberation*, Aldershot: Ashgate, 2003.

2 Stanley Hauerwas, *Character and the Christian Life: A Study in Christian Ethics*, 2nd edn, Notre Dame: University of Notre Dame Press, 1995.

3 Stanley Hauerwas, *Dispatches from the Front: Theological Engagements with the Secular*, Durham and London: Duke University Press, 1994, pp. 21–2.

4 René Descartes, *A Discourse on Method*, London: J. M. Dent & Sons Ltd, 1946, p. 79.

5 For a more in-depth description of these thinkers see my *The Ecclesiology of Stanley Hauerwas*, pp. 37–57.

6 *Character and the Christian Life.*

7 *Vision and Virtue: Essays in Christian Ethical Reflection*, Notre Dame: University of Notre Dame Press, 1981.

8 *Vision and Virtue*, pp. 14 and 30–6.

9 Stanley Hauerwas, with Richard Bondi and David B. Burrell, *Truthfulness and Tragedy: Further Investigations into Christian Ethics*, 2nd edn, Notre Dame: University of Notre Dame Press, 1985.

10 *Truthfulness and Tragedy*, pp. 15–39.

11 *A Community of Character: Toward a Constructive Christian Social Ethic*, 4th edn, Notre Dame: University of Notre Dame Press, 1986.

12 *A Community of Character*, p. 37.

13 *A Community of Character*, pp. 96, 149–50.

14 Stanley Hauerwas, 'Must a Patient Be a Person, or My Uncle Charlie Is Not Much of a Person But He Is Still My Uncle Charlie', *Connecticut Medicine*, 39/12, 1975, pp. 815–17.

15 *The Peaceable Kingdom: A Primer in Christian Ethics*, 3rd edn, Notre Dame and London: University of Notre Dame Press, 1986.

16 *A Better Hope: Resources for a Church Confronting Capitalism, Democracy and Postmodernity*, Grand Rapids: Brazos Press, 2000, pp. 71–115.

17 *The Peaceable Kingdom*, pp. 15–16.

18 *The Peaceable Kingdom*, p. 102.

19 *Performing the Faith: Bonhoeffer and the Practice of Nonviolence*, London: SPCK, 2004, pp. 170–200.

20 *In Good Company: The Church as Polis*, Notre Dame: University of Notre Dame Press, 1995, p. 58.

21 William H. Willimon and Stanley Hauerwas, with Scott C. Sage, *Lord Teach Us: The Lord's Prayer and the Christian Life*, Nashville: Abingdon Press, 1996, p. 89.

22 *Dispatches from the Front*, p. 83. For essays on these themes see Stanley Hauerwas, *A Better Hope.*

23 On Hauerwas's ecology see *In Good Company*, pp. 185–97. On natural theology see *With the Grain of the Universe: The Church's Witness and Natural Theology*, London: SCM, 2001.

24 *Christian Existence Today: Essays on Church, World and Living in Between*, Durham NC: The Labyrinth Press, 1988.

25 *Christian Existence Today*, pp. 47–65.

26 *Christian Existence Today*, pp. 111–32.

27 *Christian Existence Today*, p. 107. See also 'Liturgical Shape of the Christian Life: Teaching Christian Ethics as Worship', in *In Good Company*, pp. 153–68.

28 *Against the Nations: War and Survival in a Liberal Society*, Notre Dame: University of Notre Dame Press, 1992, pp. 6–7.

29 *Against the Nations*, pp. 21–45.

30 *Unleashing the Scripture: Freeing the Bible from Captivity to America*, Nashville: Abingdon Press, 1993, pp. 9, 15.

31 See the essays in *In Good Company.*

32 *Suffering Presence: Theological Reflections on Medicine, the Mentally Handicapped and the Church*, Edinburgh: T. & T. Clark, 1988 and *Naming the Silences: God, Medicine and the Problem of Suffering*, 2nd edn, Edinburgh: T. & T. Clark, 1993.

33 Hans Frei, *The Eclipse of Biblical Narrative: A Study in Eighteenth and Nineteenth Century Hermeneutics*, New Haven and London: Yale University Press, 1974, and George A. Lindbeck, *The Nature of Doctrine, Religion in a Postliberal Age*, Philadelphia: Westminster Press, 1984.

34 *Sanctify Them in the Truth: Holiness Exemplified*, Edinburgh: T. & T. Clark, 1998, p. 5.

35 Stanley Hauerwas and William H. Willimon, *Resident Aliens: Life in the Christian Colony*, Nashville: Abingdon Press, 1989, p. 55.

36 *In Good Company*, p. 58.

37 *A Better Hope*, p. 9.

38 *A Better Hope*, p. 24.

39 See Nigel Biggar's summary in Mark Thiessen Nation and Samuel Wells (eds), *Faithfulness and Fortitude: In Conversation with the Theological Ethics of Stanley Hauerwas*, Edinburgh: T. & T. Clark, 2000, p. 152.

40 Brad J. Kallenberg, *Ethics as Grammar: Changing the Postmodern Subject*, Notre Dame: University of Notre Dame Press, 2001, p. 156.

2

Narrating Holiness

Hauerwas regards holiness as central to discipleship and to the mission of the Church. He identifies the tangible community of faith as vital to the ongoing witness of the Christian faith. Christianity is not an ideology. Instead, it is a people performing the faith in contemporary life. Through such performances Christians offer an empirical challenge to the corrosive effects of abstract and individualistic idealism present in western societies. In contrast they are contingent and communal signs of salvation. Living holiness therefore is the critical witness of the Church and is the condition for grasping the call of God in contemporary life. Such witness tells a story which is embodied in a society. In this chapter I will explore Hauerwas's views on the Church's narrative. In the next I will look more closely at his ecclesial politics.

Holiness and story

Hauerwas began his project by trying to recover a distinctively Christian vision of reality: a way of seeing life that only Christians could embody. Sight, however, simply describes and, as such, can imply an abstract spectator. As his project matures, therefore, Hauerwas replaces sight with narrative as the focus of his attention. Narrative is more than simply description or the recounting of facts, it is about formation through time, or the generation of Christian character, as part of a distinctive community. Hauerwas is attracted to narrative as a way of representing the Christian story for a variety of reasons which he believes escape the problems of the Enlightenment ethics discussed in Chapter 1.

- Narrative enables character to be displayed, since it takes into account the development of human identity through time and as part of particular communities. The self is a story and is embedded in a social story. Narrative also makes casuistry fruitful in a way that Karl Barth's highly particular and intuitive understanding of special ethics rejected. We can trace the character of people through the disclosure of their stories and learn from these disclosures, particularly when looking for good exemplars of faith. The saints matter to Hauerwas.
- Narrative means that ethics pays attention to the embodied and situated agent rather than simply to the quandary. The way the agent sees the quandary is through the formative influence of the story which this agent inhabits. Neither the situation nor the ethical agent are stable. The interpreted situation is itself located in the dynamics of time and place while the interpreter is being formed by the living story of their community to see in a way that is particular to this narrative and the community.
- Narrative locates ethical agency in communal settings which provide a more robust resource for truthful sight/interpretation than the individualism of the Enlightenment spectator. This diminishes the self-deception of individualism flagged up by thinkers such as the 'masters of suspicion', Iris Murdoch and Alasdair MacIntyre.
- Narrative enables Hauerwas to transcend the 'fact: value' divorce at the heart of liberal thinking since narrative reveals that human character is being formed and that character disposes agents to identify 'facts' in ways relative to the stories of their communities which themselves reflect the values embedded in the practices of their core communities. Facts are therefore infected with values, and what counts as a fact will depend upon which narrative an agent is living within.
- Narrative integrates the particular and the universal without the one destroying the other. In telling a story, it is the particulars of that story which give it its substance and together suggest its shape. Yet the shape is also anticipated by the process of telling the story since all stories presume an ending which locates the particulars of that story.[1]

Nevertheless, although Hauerwas recognizes the fruitfulness of a narrative approach to ethics, he is not trying to replace a theory of human consciousness as the foundation for secure knowledge with another foundational theory. Indeed, in 'The Narrative Turn Thirty Years Later' he expresses reserve at being called a narrative theologian rather than simply a Christian one.[2] Such an approach makes a literary theory more fundamental than theology in understanding the ways of God with the world and effectively uses narrative as the basis for a general anthropology. It also uses narrative as an apologetic strategy for making Christianity intelligible to modern liberal thought. Instead, Hauerwas is drawn to narrative because this is how God's ways are given to us. The story is a gift rather than a human construction. In consequence he believes that Christian theology is unavoidably narrative in character and seeks to show the truth about God through describing the narrative evoked by the performances of the Christian community's practices. Worship as the performance of the central complex of church practices is a form of poetics, a way of shaping the imagination of a community so that it can inhabit the ongoing story of God faithfully.[3]

Holiness and a truthful story

We saw in Chapter 1 that Hauerwas's project is part of the post-Enlightenment debate about knowing truth. In reaction to the apparent fog of theological controversy held to have caused the seventeenth-century century Wars of Religion in Europe, Enlightenment thinkers tried to found a secure and true knowledge of reality in mental rationality (Descartes) or empirical rationality (Hume), both of which treated the human thinker as central. Such an approach was also encouraged by the advances in the natural sciences, based as they were on apparently universally agreed spectator modes of observation and experiment, rather than upon conflicting arguments about texts and tradition. Hauerwas is profoundly sceptical about the security of such foundations for establishing truth. Indeed, he comments 'I have a well-deserved reputation for being an unapologetic Enlightenment basher.'[4] Like other critics of the Enlightenment, he challenges the notion of an objective spectator view of reality which can offer us secure access to universal truth. Instead, as embedded and temporal thinkers we are unable to stand outside what we seek to understand and therefore cannot survey everything in a way that can secure universal agreement about what constitutes truth even in the natural sciences. Instead, discerning truth is more complex and involves the testing out of claims to truth in different areas of human understanding according to the character of what is being explored. This cannot be achieved simply by listening to contemporary truth claims and their justification. It also involves seeing how coherently these claims are sustained through time and in the lives of the communities which assert them. Truth is discovered through listening carefully to stories and by attending to the sort of communities that these stories generate. It involves being able to give convincing reasons to justify the claims being made, takes account of how illuminating these reasons are and how impressively they interpret the situation or issues. This implies that there will be rival truth claims by rival traditions of thought and practice that cannot be resolved through an appeal to a mythical universal human spectator judge. Consequently Hauerwas holds that truth claims convince when they give the best account of the evidence, are more persuasive than their competitors and when they engender communities whose life coheres with the character of the truth claims they assert.

Since the Enlightenment project does not represent a universally agreed approach to discerning truth and reality, its claim to provide a timeless and universally agreed way of grasping truth is false. Instead, the project represents a particular contextual tradition making contestable truth claims alongside other rival claimants. Given his rejection of the Enlightenment's universalist pretensions and his re-description of Enlightenment thought as one truth-claiming story among many, Hauerwas deliberately presents the Christian tradition as a rival narrative whose plausibility is established not by appealing to abstract universally accessible norms but by displaying a people whose character indicates the truthfulness of their claims.[5] It is the community living the story that will enable that story to be open to judgement. Such judgement, however, is not the judgement of the abstract spectator since no one exists as a detached spectator. Instead, judgement takes place within the experience of what is being evaluated and within communities of practice. This means that Christian truth claims will be evaluated in terms of how convincingly they can justify themselves, offer illumination to life, exhibit a plausible coherence and have explanatory capacity. Can the truth claims that Christians make withstand scrutiny? Does the story that Christians tell about reality shed light on that reality in a persuasive manner and in a way that helps us to understand reality more fully? Is this story coherent? Does this story explain our experience of reality in a more satisfying manner than its rivals, particularly when dealing with the unexpected and undesired? In short, discerning the plausibility of truth claims has a very tangible and public character.

The credibility of the Christian story is inextricably related to the character of the Christian community, since the way Christians live should cohere with the story they tell. Their walk should evoke their talk. The truthfulness of Christian claims, accordingly, will also display itself in the way this story has universal scope and yet does not destroy the integrity of particular details in the process.[6] Such living holiness involves inhabiting a story in which the vulnerable are treasured and the tragic is not denied. Furthermore, whereas the Enlightenment story revolves around singular human consciousness and is prey to the limitations and fluidity of finite human perspective, the Church's story underwrites its claim to participate in God through being a community of all peoples.[7] It speaks, thereby, of the universal reach of this story as the story of God who alone has the capacity to engage all while respecting the particularity of all. The truth about God, the world and human living emerges by interpreting the story which is 'told' as the Church embodies this story in its ongoing living. It is truthfulness on the way.[8]

The narrative character of Christian ethics means that they are always open to new truths as the Church participates in the divine story. Hence Hauerwas finds himself wrestling with issues such as abortion, euthanasia, disability, sexuality and peaceableness in ways which have to take account of the dynamics of Christian formation, expanding vision and changing insights. For example, when wrestling with gay issues he finds resources for making headway in a sensitive area by reflecting on the theme of Christian friendship, particularly for the stranger. If early Christians discovered that friendship in Christ with Gentiles opened up new theological horizons and consequently asked them to re-configure the boundaries of salvation, so the fact of finding friendship with gays and lesbians raises similar implications for him. This is especially so since baptism indicates that the primary calling of the whole Church is to be reproductive baptismally rather than biologically.[9] Nevertheless he is also aware of other issues involved in framing the debate. He is worried that inclusive Christians take their bearings from a contemporary and abstract understanding of inclusivity rather than beginning with those church practices such as baptism and marriage which interpret promiscuity and friendship from within the Christian story.[10] These indicate that marriage is fundamentally about the welcome and care of children rather than the romantic and emotive needs of adults. Marriage is a practice 'wherein the goal of sex finds material embodiment in the gift of children'.[11] Baptism then re-identifies these children as the Church's children and means that all Christians have a parenting role whether married or not. This distinction between marriage and friendship means that parenting is the responsibility of the whole Church, since through baptismal parenting, children are befriended by the adult community. Nevertheless Hauerwas remains concerned that capitalism makes all consumers rather than producers and that the consumerist approach to sex predominant in North America is about short-term commitment to play rather than lifelong commitment to the task of procreation. It is consequently self-centred rather than other-centred. This means that although he has some reserve about gay relationships since they are biologically non-reproductive, the major problem for Christian ethics is not same-sex friendships but heterosexual relationships which refuse to live up to their reproductive calling expressed through the practice of lifelong marriage. Gay marriage may be a misnomer, but understanding gay relationships as about faithful friendship may be more hopeful.

Holiness and a timeful story

Hauerwas's work is presented predominantly in essays or sermons rather than as a systematic treatise. This has caused some to doubt whether he can offer the sort of coherence which a truthful narrative demands. Any careful reading of his work, however, will reveal a journey whose story can be told intelligibly. As he says, 'I refuse to be a systematic theologian, but that does not mean what I write is not interconnected.'[12] This interconnected account of truthfulness is not an abstract or systematic account of what is true, since our reflecting is never complete or outside of time. Rather, as he comments, 'I do not have a finished theological system, nor do I believe in such a thing … my suspicion is that the desire to have such a system may indicate the theologians' lack of faith in the Church.'[13] Church is a community living through time and within which are located the practices which carry the theological convictions of that community. The theological task, therefore, has to engage with the embodied and temporal Church rather than with purely abstract ideas about the Church, God or truth. Hauerwas's style is itself a reflection of the fact that theology, like all other disciplines, is reflection in process. Essays and sermons are by their nature interim reflections on an ongoing journey rather than definitive expositions of abstract truths. Coherence, therefore, emerges through time rather than simply by getting everything together in one great work. In contrast to the Enlightenment quest to transcend the limitations of time and place, his reflections on the theological significance of the Church are explicitly situated in time and place.

To narrate the story of the Christian community's holy living entails learning the language of the community. The Church, as a distinctively Christian community, has its own language with a variety of dialects. Telling the story of God embodied in the Church means learning the Christian language as it is spoken by the Church and becoming a competent, fluent speaker of that language. Character, community and speech are therefore all related to one another. One cannot learn to talk unless one is part of the body whose language one is articulating. Again, holiness and story are interdependent since 'the truthfulness of Christian convictions depends on the witness of truthful lives'.[14] Hence the worship of the Church forms its participants into a Christian language which describes reality in terms of the ongoing story of God's grace. Gathering to worship is about learning the grammatical rules for speaking this language and telling this story in life.

Living holiness within the story of God's ways with the world involves remembering the past faithfully. This is not about holding the Church's story to account before the bar of a fictitious universal history of the kind emerging from the Enlightenment. Instead, it is about recognizing the effect of the past upon the contemporary Church and about the way in which telling the story of that past enables the contemporary Church to live truthfully. The United States is particularly prone to fostering amnesia since it was a society configured to forgetting the past in order to forge a new society of individuals. Consequently its citizens have no sense of their distinctive histories, presume a singular view of history, and seek to seduce others to regard this particular American history as the history of all. In this situation 'the Church is God's good memory for the world' since it is a community which remembers that its sins are forgiven.[15] It does not try to forget the past but to allow that past to be redeemed through this forgiveness. As such, Hauerwas believes it represents a community whose remembered story enables Christians to resist the careless presentism and amnesia of contemporary American capitalism.

Holiness and a catholic story

For Hauerwas, narrative is ultimately dependent upon holiness, and holiness is formed through the disciplines or practices of worship and service. The performance and narrative of contemporary discipleship of necessity includes the story of Christian ancestors, since the Christian story did not begin with its contemporary agents. In addition, the catholicity or universal embrace of this story is only seen when this narrative includes the stories of the marginal and superficially insignificant. God's story, to which the Church bears witness, is universal or catholic in so far as it embraces and redeems all creation. It excludes no strangers since through grace all strangers become friends in God's story. The stories of those most easily excluded from the stories of the powerful become the indicators of the truthful character of the Christian account of reality. This is one more reason why Hauerwas regards the post-Enlightenment story as an excluding sectarian narrative in the service of privileged and powerful elites since that story has no place for the weak or 'abnormal'. In the post-Enlightenment story these human beings are either squeezed into the idealistic norm or, in the case of the unborn child or demented elderly, actively destroyed through abortion and effective euthanasia. In so doing the Enlightenment displays a totalitarian approach which regards anything and anyone strange as a threat.[16] Such human beings challenge the singular, universal ideals and timeless norms which the Enlightenment project believed it had discovered. In contrast, the Christian story is hospitable to the outsider, the 'other' or the 'different' since its core plot involves God in Christ embracing the strangeness of created human flesh mired in sin in order to love and redeem it.

Holiness and a reality story

At the heart of the Church's story is the conviction that God is love. Yet this is not an abstract or plastic vision of love prey to the sentimentality of a particular generation. Rather, it is rooted in the story of the love of Christ held in the Church's memory and embodied in the lives of Christians.[17] Here is a story which equips those who embody it with the capacity to face the agony of the world rather than trying to screen it out. It enables them to acknowledge the irreducible particularity of people's lives, since suffering is always somebody's suffering rather than suffering in general.[18] Nevertheless Hauerwas believes that the way Jesus responds to his suffering indicates the pathway for Christian discipleship. The Church is the body of Christ and shares in the narrating of his story. Drawing upon the work of John Howard Yoder, Hauerwas derives a social ethic from the particular life of Christ precisely because the Church now is his body in contemporary societies.[19] The story of Jesus is found not so much in texts as in the lives of Christians since 'Jesus did not have a social ethic ... his story is a social ethic'.[20] How Christians live is informed by the cruciform story of Jesus which inscribes their own identities and indicates how they are to trust God with their lives. Such trust may only be vindicated after death, which is why martyrdom is the most explicit indication of Christian trust. Hauerwas finds that this sort of trust is exemplified in the story of Thomas More. Here was a public officer willing to stand against the pretensions of King Henry VIII's state because he was convinced that this threatened his primary loyalty to the story of God mediated by the Church. The result of his witness was that he was executed and the meaning of his story was offered to God. A counter-story is that of the Nazi Albert Speer, whose lack of a theological story gave him no basis for resisting Hitler's commands. Hauerwas sees in Speer the effects of liberalism, since without a divinely accountable story the singular human agent is powerless to resist the powers that seek to dominate life.[21]

Knowing when the Christian story invites this quality of trust is less about thinking things through and more about living as a holy community. Such common living holiness ensures that temptations to individualistic interpretations of the story are disciplined by community participation.[22] The body holds together the interpretative possibilities of its story. There will inevitably be a variety of interpretations about how to live the story in particular contexts and eras.[23] However, these will still remain accountable to the whole Church even if some disputes may have to await God's final judgement rather than being resolved by human agreement.

Furthermore, the story's tradition both indicates and disposes the development of contemporary discipleship since it acts as a sort of guide, enabling new challenges to be negotiated in a manner consonant with the holiness of the God witnessed to in the past. 'The gospel is a story that gives you a way of being in the world.'[24] It is not about interesting ideas so much as about practical holy living which witnesses to the Christian God who is named and storied rather than being an abstract concept.[25] Accordingly Hauerwas insists 'the only relevant critical examination of Christian beliefs may be one which begins by attending to the lived lives'.[26] Indeed, it will be the living holiness of the Church, which displays what Jesus means today.[27]

Holiness and a scriptural story

The Scriptures, for Hauerwas, in spite of being at the heart of the Christian story, do not exhaust that story. Their internal plurality as Gospels, histories, law, letters, proverbs and the like, which belong within the overall story of Scripture, together with the diverse embodiments of Church across the globe and in history, indicate that together 'our stories become part of the story of the kingdom (making) Jesus' story a many sided tale'.[28] Similarly it is the existence of the Church which underscores the authority of Scripture, since without this enfleshed community, Scripture would simply be another series of ancient texts for academics.[29] The reading of the Bible as Scripture, rather than as ancient biblical texts, is only properly undertaken in and as the Church. This reading is disciplined and given its primary context by liturgy rather than by the academy or solitary student. Performance of the liturgy trains Christians to become competent interpreters of the story. In such contexts Scripture is revelatory, since as the community gathers to worship and listen to Scripture, their particular vocation within the mission of God is clarified. Equally Christian discipleship involves improvising upon the scriptural stories in the context of contemporary living. The Church is the community which trains Christians in the skills that enable such improvisation to occur faithful to the story.[30] This means that the canon of Scripture is not a finished product since the story it witnesses to is being realized as people become part of the Church and augment the story. There is therefore no singular meaning of Scripture, since their meaning is relative to where and with whom the Church is on its journey. The story of God's grace is an ongoing story about the transformation of sinners into a holy community.

Holiness and theological story

Imitating Christ is not about reconstructing a definitive historical account of the life of Jesus in the first century so much as about walking in the way of the Lord as Jesus and Israel did.[31] For Israel this meant living in the relationship established by the Exodus story. For Christians it is about living in the relationship with God and creation established by Jesus, in his life, death and resurrection.[32] It is not an exhaustive story of reality so much as one about God's saving work.[33] A part of the Christian theologian's task, as a servant of the Church, must therefore be to keep reminding the Church about the implications of its narrative. Likewise the preacher, as another officer of the Church, exercises a particular theological task in the sermon, since here is a communal or common contextual reflection upon the challenge of the narrative embodied in the lives of those gathered. The sermon is a 'pause for reflection' in the flow of community life during which the community listens attentively to its critical texts within the horizon of its contemporary vocation. A sermon is fleshly faith in focus. The holiness of the Church is therefore crucial in the interpretative process. Faithful practice and the performance of Christian living forms truthful and competent interpreters more than intellectual ability and textual dexterity alone. It is Scripture in the Church, which informs the interpretative life of that Church.[34] This is necessarily specific and particular given the embodied character of the Church in time and space and cannot simply be left to the abstract individual beloved of post-Enlightenment thought.

Holiness and particular stories

Abstract notions of Church have to defer in Hauerwas's opinion to tangible Churches such as Broadway Methodist Church and Aldersgate Methodist Church of which he was a member.[35] Formation in this sort of community, webbed as it is into the wider Christian tradition, evokes a distinctive reading of the Scriptures and an understanding of the vocational suggestiveness of these Scriptural stories. Much of what is evoked will be relatively mundane by the world's standards. Yet these mundane practices and activities, the 'bread and butter' of discipleship, are the gestures which most remarkably indicate the presence of God's grace in this community. It is in the details of such living holiness that the truthfulness of the story is carried and narrated by the Church. The details are where particular elements of the Body of Christ act as particular apologies for the grace of God in ways that display trust in God's care.[36] In particular a simple action such as going to Church acts as a major political statement, since it acknowledges God as sovereign rather than any other principalities or powers.[37]

Holiness and a performed story

The Christian faith as story reflects a distinctive communal performance shaped by the active agency of God within that community and mediated by the Spirit through worship. In this sense it is a story given to us to live rather than an apologetic strategy to make Christianity relevant to modernity.[38] This story performed by Christians is about peaceableness and indicates a very different sort of community compared with the ancient polis or the modern state.[39] The latter are premised upon human power and agency, whether this be the self-sufficient male of Aristotle or the coercive power of the modern state. Both consequently tell a story in which violence and the destruction of difference triumph.

In contrast, Hauerwas believes that the Church's story is peaceable because it is a community whose life is infused with Christ's peaceable presence as promised in Matthew 28.20. As such, its claims are not imperialistic since they are expressed through invitation rather than coercion. Hence the 'Christian community is ... a sociological order; its beliefs and practices arise out of a way of life together.'[40] It is the presence of such a community that enables and embodies the ongoing story as a witness to the gospel. Indeed, 'the community of the Church is constitutive of the gospel proclamation'.[41] Christian speech should reflect rather than determine a community's character. Worship, evangelism and ethics similarly belong together since they are about fostering holy communities which sign and speak of salvation.[42] However, this does not imply the ecclesiastical captivity of God.[43] Hauerwas will countenance no abstract doctrine of God since this renders 'God' prey to ideological captivity by abstract theologians, which is even worse. Like the German theologian Karl Barth, he is hostile to any attempt to put God into our hands.[44] Rather, the fact of there being a Church which speaks about God and in so speaking finds itself caught up in that about which it speaks is critical. The key is to show by our lives 'that our existence and the existence of the universe are unintelligible if the God found in Jesus Christ is not God'.[45] Christian speech is our witness to God as well as the revelation of our status as creatures, even though the full story will not be told until the *parousia*. However, even in the interim this offers the possibility of a substantial challenge to the late modern narrative which purports to describe nature without need of God. It also enables the Church's story to accept truths about the creation mediated by other disciplines, since the Christian story recognizes that God's Kingdom embraces all, whether this is acknowledged by them or not.

Holiness and a world story

The Church's story therefore remains open to the future, since although its core plot pivots around Christ and includes all the stories of the faithful ancestors, there remain others who will become part of the pilgrim people through baptism. Their stories will augment the existing narrative. In addition, the coherence of the Christian story embodied in the Church is a missional sign since it offers to the world (that is to those who as yet do not believe) a divine story about themselves. Furthermore, the coherence of the Christian story embodied in the Church is a missional sign since it offers to the world a divine story about themselves. It speaks of the world as that community which God is inviting to join his people and thereby discover their true identity as God's friends. Without this divine story the world has no story to give it meaning, since there is no meta-narrative within which its diverse and conflicting voices can be related. The world needs the Church to make sense of itself and to tell stories, such as those about the Shoah/Holocaust or the Jonestown massacre, in the light of its Christian understanding about God to set alongside those of the Jewish community. Such stories may well be sobering ones for the Church to reflect upon as well.

Holiness and a plural story

Hauerwas is well aware of the diversities of Christian practice throughout the Church. The Christian story is a many-sided tale with a variety of ecclesial expressions. In part, this is due to the arguments of history. However, it is also reflective of the contingent and embedded character of human living. The Christian story is lived contextually, which implies a degree of ecclesial plurality. Nevertheless the variety of Christian communities cannot tell their own stories without including one another in their accounts. There is therefore a narrative ecumenism which underscores the embodied and catholic character of this community.[46] Christian beliefs, though, are not self-referential or self-justifying. God is the author of this story. Yet the universal sign of God's presence in the Church, witnessed by its catholic character as a community across generations, genders and geography, enables it to test the plausibility of those claiming to be part of the Church. This does not mean that a complete resolution of these claims can be achieved before the *parousia* or Second Advent of Christ. Yet because the final outcome of the story is in the hands of God, this is not destructive of the truthfulness of the story to which they bear provisional and fallible witness. Nevertheless, all this reminds the Church that no particular narrative is the exhaustive rendition of the story. The *parousia* is the context for such a rendition. In the interim, provisionality is the order of the day.

Conclusion

Hauerwas explores the Church as a story about God and the world. It is a story which, he maintains, is told in the presence and practices of those communities which worship Jesus as Lord in contemporary society. The story is made up of several narratives as different Christian communities live the gospel in their diverse contexts. Yet the story is held together by the common identity of these communities as Church given to them in baptism by God and nourished by God through worship. The holiness of these communities speaks provisionally and fallibly of the character of the God they worship. The theology that these narratives make possible helps Christians to see their discipleship within the horizon of God's rich and gracious dealings with the world. As Christians witness through the holiness of their life together, they enable others to hear and, above all, see the grace of God at work. In a media-saturated, virtual reality society, a community as tangible as the Church stands out increasingly as a beacon pointing to a deeper story than that on offer. In the next chapter I want to explore further the way the Church embodies a narrative sign to the grace of God in the world.

Questions

- In what ways has Hauerwas helped you to understand the place of story in Christian discipleship?
- How could the Church tell its story better?
- How does your local Christian community narrate something of the Christian story?
- How should the Church listen to the stories of other truth claimants?

Further reading

Frei, Hans, *The Eclipse of Biblical Narrative: A Study in Eighteenth and Nineteenth Century Hermeneutics*, New Haven and London: Yale University Press, 1974.

Hauerwas, Stanley with Richard Bondi and David B. Burrell, *Truthfulness and Tragedy: Further Investigations into Christian Ethics*, 2nd edn, Notre Dame: University of Notre Dame Press, 1985.

Hauerwas, Stanley, *Naming the Silences: God, Medicine and the Problem of Suffering*, 2nd edn, Edinburgh: T. & T. Clark, 1993.

—— *Unleashing the Scripture: Freeing the Bible from Captivity to America*, Nashville: Abingdon Press, 1993.

Hauerwas, Stanley and L. Gregory Jones (eds), *Why Narrative?*, Grand Rapids: Eerdmans, 1989.

Hunsinger, George and William C. Placher (eds), *Theology and Narrative: Selected Essays*, Oxford: Oxford University Press, 1993.

Lindbeck, George A., *The Nature of Doctrine: Religion in a Postliberal Age*, Philadelphia: Westminster Press, 1984.

Loughlin, Gerald, *Telling God's Story: Bible, Church and Narrative Theology*, Cambridge: Cambridge University Press, 1996.

Nelson, Paul, *Narrative and Morality: A Theological Inquiry*, University Park and London: Pennsylvania State University Press, 1987.

Stroup, George W., *The Promise of Narrative Theology*, London: SCM, 1981.

Thiemann, Ronald F., *Revelation as Theology: The Gospel as Narrated Promise*, Notre Dame: University of Notre Dame Press, 1985.

Notes

1 For an extended discussion on narrative see Stanley Hauerwas and L. Gregory Jones (eds), *Why Narrative?*, Grand Rapids: Eerdmans, 1989.

2 'The Narrative Turn Thirty Years Later', in *Performing the Faith: Bonhoeffer and the Practice of Nonviolence*, London: SPCK, 2004, pp. 136–47.

3 *Performing the Faith*, p. 154.

4 *A Better Hope: Resources for a Church Confronting Capitalism, Democracy and Postmodernity*, Grand Rapids: Brazos Press, 2000, p. 23.

5 Stanley Hauerwas with Richard Bondi and David B. Burrell, *Truth-*

fulness and Tragedy: Further Investigations into Christian Ethics, 2nd edn, Notre Dame: University of Notre Dame Press, 1985, pp. 15–39.

6 *Christian Existence Today: Essays on Church, World and Living in Between*, Durham NC: The Labyrinth Press, 1988, pp. 47–65.

7 *Sanctify Them in the Truth: Holiness Exemplified*, Edinburgh: T. & T. Clark, 1998, p. 192 and *A Better Hope*, pp. 35–46.

8 *Sanctify Them*, pp. 114–15.

9 Stanley Hauerwas, 'Gay Friendship: A Thought Experiment in Catholic Moral Theology', in *Sanctify Them*, pp. 117–18 and 'Resisting Capitalism: On Marriage and Homosexuality', in *A Better Hope*, pp. 47–51.

10 'Resisting Capitalism: On Marriage and Homosexuality', in *A Better Hope*, pp. 47–51.

11 *A Better Hope*, p. 49.

12 Mark Thiessen Nation and Samuel Wells (eds), *Faithfulness and Fortitude: In Conversation with the Theological Ethics of Stanley Hauerwas*, Edinburgh: T. & T. Clark, 2000, p. 310.

13 *Wilderness Wanderings: Probing Twentieth-Century Theology and Philosophy*, Boulder: Westview Press, 1997, p. 5.

14 *The State of the University: Academic Knowledges and the Knowledge of God*, Oxford: Blackwell, 2007, p. 3.

15 *A Better Hope*, p. 152.

16 *A Community of Character: Toward a Constructive Christian Social Ethic*, 4th edn, Notre Dame: University of Notre Dame Press, 1986, pp. 129–52.

17 *Vision and Virtue: Essays in Christian Ethical Reflection*, Notre Dame: University of Notre Dame Press, 1981, pp. 111–26.

18 *Naming the Silences: God, Medicine and the Problem of Suffering*, 2nd edn, Edinburgh: T. & T. Clark, 1993.

19 John H. Yoder, *The Original Revolution: Essays in Christian Pacifism*, Scottdale: Herald Press, 1971; *The Politics of Jesus*, 2nd edn, Grand Rapids: Eerdmans, 1982 and *The Priestly Kingdom Social Ethics as Gospel*, Notre Dame: University of Notre Dame Press, 1984.

20 *A Community of Character*, p. 37.

21 *Christian Existence Today*, pp. 199–217.

22 *A Community of Character*, pp. 9–35.

23 *Christian Existence Today*, pp. 21–45.

24 *Truthfulness and Tragedy*, p. 73.

25 *Lord Teach Us: The Lord's Prayer and the Christian Life*, Nashville: Abingdon Press, 1996, p. 42.

26 *Truthfulness and Tragedy*, p. 81.

27 *A Community of Character*, p. 37.

28 *A Community of Character*, pp. 51–2.

29 *A Community of Character*, p. 53.

30 *Performing the Faith*, pp. 80–1. See also Samuel Wells, *Improvisation: The Drama of Christian Ethics*, London: SPCK, 2004.

31 *The Peaceable Kingdom: A Primer in Christian Ethics*, 3rd edn, Notre Dame and London: University of Notre Dame Press, 1986, p. 77.

32 *The Peaceable Kingdom*, p. 87.

33 'God's New Language', in *Christian Existence Today*, pp. 47–56.

34 See *Unleashing the Scripture: Freeing the Bible from Captivity to America*, Nashville: Abingdon Press, 1993.

35 *Sanctify Them*, p. xi.

36 *Christian Existence Today*, pp. 101–10.

37 Stanley Hauerwas and William H. Willimon, *Where Resident Aliens Live: Exercises for Christian Practices*, Nashville: Abingdon Press, 1996, p. 43.

38 *Performing the Faith*, pp. 136–48.

39 Stanley Hauerwas and Charles Pinches, *Christians Among the Virtues: Theological Conversations with Ancient and Modern Ethics*, Notre Dame: University of Notre Dame Press, 1997, pp. 89–112.

40 *Where Resident Aliens Live*, p. 72.

41 *With the Grain of the Universe: The Church, Witness and Natural Theology*, Grand Rapids: Brazos Press, 2001, p. 145.

42 *A Better Hope*, p. 160.

43 Linda Woodhead, 'Review of *In Good Company*', *Studies in Christian Ethics*, 10/1, 1997, 112–15, pp. 114–15.

44 *With the Grain of the Universe*, p. 164.

45 *With the Grain of the Universe*, pp. 190–1.

46 *Sanctify Them*, p. 4.

3

Embodying Holiness

In the previous chapter we saw how Hauerwas relates the way the Church lives to the way its story is narrated. Peaceableness is the hallmark of this story, and in his work on Bonhoeffer he argues that there is a necessary connection between truthfulness, non-violence and the quest for a truthful politics.[1] The story is grounded in the performance of the Church. In this sense, Hauerwas could be described as a pragmatist and a materialist, since it is the materiality of faith embodied in peaceable living that indicates the truthful character of the Church's story. Truth is displayed pragmatically through a way of life rather than by theoretical justification. Hence the role of the Church's witness is analogous to an experiment in the natural sciences. It tests the truth of Christian claims about God and the world. Similarly Christian theology goes wrong if the Church's life is wrongly configured. What the Church says flows from the character of its life rather than the other way around. This further distinguishes him from Karl Barth, whose weakness, he believes, is precisely found in his stunning intellectual achievement. Barth's *Church Dogmatics* are not dependent upon the witness of the Church but upon their intellectual coherence.[2] In contrast, Hauerwas's concern is to prevent Christianity becoming another set of ideas or abstractions that can be divorced from the condition and activity of our bodies. As he remarks,

> recent developments, which some call postmodernism, offer some extremely helpful ways for a display of holiness without a loss of the Catholic character of the church. The loss of the 'self' and the increasing appreciation of the significance of the body,

> and in particular, the body's permeability, can help recover holiness, not as an individual achievement, but as the work of the Holy Spirit building up the body of Christ.[3]

Hauerwas believes that spirituality is not what God does in some mysterious and enigmatic dimension of human consciousness but the material experience of God transforming human bodies into living sacrifices. Living holiness matters, since how Christians live together, walk together, witness together and eat together constitutes the character of the Christian witness. Indeed, 'any intelligible account of Christianity requires Christians to lead lives of holiness that make clear that the Church is integral to that project and not just a means to that end.'[4] Furthermore, the body, for Christians, is not the closet of the soul or self. Rather, the body is that permeable, relational and tangible identity which locates us within communities whose practices speak about the vision of reality they profess. Indeed, for Christians, bodies gain their true meaning and destiny by participating in the body of Christ through baptism. Thus bodies can be transformed and they represent a divine story about life. This is what being part of the body of Christ means for Christians and represents faith in flesh.[5] Such living holiness is not about making Christianity relevant to contemporary society but about challenging that society to pay attention to God as depicted in the story which the Church embodies.

In this chapter I want to explore further how Hauerwas understands the society and politics of the Church to embody holiness. For Hauerwas the shape of the Church underscores the plausibility of the gospel in late modern societies, saturated as they are by abstract rhetoric, virtual encounters and suspicion towards all claims to truthfulness. He regards these deceptions as particularly evident in North American societies and argues that the Church is one of the few communities with the resources to resist this 'America' becoming the fate of the world.[6] Indeed, he believes that the witness of the Church offers a tangible political sign of grace that can challenge the assumptions of modern America. It also distinguishes the world from the Church by revealing the former as that community which as yet does not live actively in this grace.[7]

The Church's political vocation

Hauerwas frequently uses political language to describe the Church, arguing that the story and practices of Christian worship and discipleship form the Christian community into a distinctive society with its own politics. Sanctification properly generates the polity of the Church as the Spirit forms Christians into a holy society with its own integrity.[8] In consequence he is particularly critical of theological traditions that have sought to make the Church relevant to their contemporary culture since they divest the Church of its distinctive social witness to the grace of God in the world. Indeed, one of his persistent concerns is that, in an attempt to make America Christian, liberal Protestantism ended up making Christianity American. It therefore has become increasingly difficult to distinguish between the Church and America. Consequently the Church has become invisible in America just as it did in Europe following the Constantinian Settlement.[9] In particular, as we noted in Chapter 1, he is very critical of political thought such as that of Reinhold Niebuhr, which he believes relegates the Church to an irrelevance and thereby subverts its witness as a distinctively Christian community.[10]

Arne Rasmusson has most clearly described Hauerwas's understanding of the Church's politics.[11] Contrasting Hauerwas with the German theologian, Jürgen Moltmann, Rasmusson argues that the former represents a form of theological politics whereas the latter advocates a political theology. Political theology, in contrast to theological politics, aims at a critical rapprochement with modern thinking in order to render Christianity relevant to that thought. In so doing it trades on contemporary concepts of justice, democracy and freedom, which are rooted in notions of human identity that are alien to the Christian tradition. In contrast, Hauerwas draws inspiration from the Radical Reformation tradition, which continues in contemporary Anabaptist thought, especially in the writings of John Howard Yoder. In this tradition the Church is to be an alternative society rather than a religious component of society and is to represent a practical distinctiveness which refuses to allow its identity to be dictated to by that society. Distinctively Christian living is the basis for recovering the sort of confident theological speech Karl Barth articulated but did not ground in the embodied narrative of the Church. Without this tangible witness, this speech remains rhetoric.[12] Like Yoder, Hauerwas believes that the politics of this community are characterized by the peaceableness practised by Christ since the doctrines of God and non-violence are, in his view, constitutive of each other. Without the Christian community living this peaceableness, there is no way that the world can grasp the character of God.

Hauerwas therefore regards the Church as a distinctively Christian society whose politics reflect its vocation to bear witness to the peaceable grace of God in the world. In so doing, Rasmusson believes that Hauerwas can engage ordinary Christians in a way that Moltmann's political theology, as the voice of the left-wing intellectual activist, never managed to do effectively. Moltmann's work represents theory rather than practice. Hauerwas, in contrast, believes that the practices of communal worship generate holy politics. Through liturgical formation the Church becomes an alternative to the world, since, as Christians worship, a form of life emerges reflective of the presence of Christ within them.[13] Such living holiness can resist the destructive tendencies of late modernity and draws its inspiration and language from the worshipping practices of the Church. Hence the Church is a community committed to a costly and truthful remembering of the past amidst late modern cultures disposed to forget that past. For example, Christians cannot accept no-fault reconciliation initiatives, since they silence the wounds of the past and ignore the cries of those seeking revenge. Christian remembering also disturbs and challenges the American ideal of freedom, which Hauerwas regards as freedom for money and from memory. He argues that America's attempt to escape from the religious turbulence of Europe was achieved by establishing capitalism as its effective religion and domesticating formal religion in the process. The licentious and fragmentary character of late modern capitalism has effectively subverted any sense of common community among Americans, rendering social relations increasingly abstract and conflictual. This contrasts with the way poverty in catholic Ireland has actually sustained a richer community life across that society, although recently this has also been increasingly subverted by the effects of capitalism.[14] Faced with the acidic effects of late modern capitalism, the Church represents a temporal and tangible sign of human community resourced by the work of God within it. As an enfleshed community rather than a collection of timeless ideas, it is a sign which Hauerwas believes to be 'the necessary condition for the proclamation of the gospel in a world that no longer privileges Christianity'.[15]

The Church's freedom

All this protects the freedom of the Church from colonization by the political legacy of the Enlightenment which we noted in Chapter 1. As Hauerwas says, 'My problem has never been with secular political liberals but rather with the widespread assumption shared by many Christians, that political liberalism ought to shape the agenda, if not the very life, of the Church.'[16] This freedom is essential for the Church's mission, since unless the Church can be seen to embody its rhetoric, its witness disappears. This is why peaceableness is so critical: peaceableness which is not abstract pacifism, but the way the Church lives in Christ's peace and thereby acts as a sign of the agenda of God for creation. Such peaceableness represents a challenge to the intrinsic violence of modern liberal political orders. These are violent because they are based upon a view of human identity which assumes that each individual is fundamentally the same. Thus whatever distinguishes people is peripheral to their common human identity. Social coherence requires that these differences must be downplayed or diminished and is achieved either by stressing common norms, to the detriment of those who do not immediately represent them, or by rendering differences marginal. As a result, religious communities are tolerated in liberal societies so long as they accept the latter's right to police them and don't challenge the system.

Policing and normalizing are strategies of liberal fascism since the rhetoric of freedom masks an effective imposition of arbitrary control. Liberal societies represent a contradiction between the rhetoric of freedom (liberal) and their effective totalitarianism (normalization), whereas the Church properly embodies an alternative polity whose agenda is drawn from the peaceable practices of Christ within it. This tension means that Christians will find that faithful living in late modern societies is increasingly uncomfortable.[17] Yet this is the gift of the Church to the world as it embodies the contrast between following Christ and following other ways.[18] Such peaceableness does not worry about ensuring the Church's survival or indeed ensuring that the Church is effective in the world's terms. Survivalism and effectiveness involve trying to keep control of the Church's destiny rather than living faithfully with God and trusting that God holds the future for both Church and world. Indeed, since the destiny of the cosmos has already been indicated by the resurrection of Jesus, the Church can confidently get on with its task of patiently witnessing to this victory. Through evangelism it can invite others to join in celebrating the fruits of Christ's achievements rather than frantically trying to get enough people into its pews to pay the bills.

The Church's peaceableness

War

Hauerwas is aware that his theological politics is a minority perspective within the Christian tradition. While most Christians deplore war, the dominant Christian tradition in European and North American Christianity has been persuaded by the just-war approach to conflict. Admittedly this is about relative peaceableness, since it seeks to limit possibilities for inter-state conflict rather than to bless such conflict. However, like Yoder, Hauerwas believes that the logic of Jesus' life, death and resurrection challenges this theory. Jesus' life, death and resurrection embody and bring about the eschatological kingdom, or peaceable reign of God, and infuse this within the life of the Church. Hence, to advocate any form of violence fails to recognize what the Church is and the new era within which the Church lives.[19] This is why his argument with the just-war ethicist, Paul Ramsey, is really an argument about eschatology. First, war, especially nuclear war, represents a rival eschatology to this peaceable eschatological kingdom since it assumes that human rather than divine agency will determine the end of the world. Second, the threat to use nuclear weapons as a form of deterrence is rooted in a commitment to survival at any cost. Yet such survivalism is an expression of practical atheism and has no confidence that God's ending is one that Christians can trust with patience. Third, nuclear warfare is an indiscriminate form of warfare whose legitimacy according to just-war criteria is mystified by the manipulative possibilities of modern media. Fourth, the just-war tradition is an explicitly Christian tradition rooted in a Christian understanding of justice and peace. It is therefore not a practice which makes sense beyond its Christian origins and consequently cannot provide the liberal state, let alone the world, with a rationale for even a limited war.[20] In effect, each of these realities makes it very difficult for Christians to use just-war criteria to argue for any form of war. Indeed, to do so will represent a major threat to the faithful witness of the Church. Furthermore, since God has the destiny of the cosmos in his hands, Christians no longer need be terrified of threats such as the nuclear bomb. Instead, in the face of such a threat they display small gestures and mundane commitments, such as having children or caring for an elderly relative, visiting the sick or going to Church as a witness to the freedom such trust brings.[21] In so doing they exhibit the Church's doctrine of God.[22] Hence whereas liberal societies find war to be the basis for their social cohesion and internal peace, Christians discover that the Church is the sign of what God has said about war. since it represents a community of difference and hope held peaceably together by God. [23]

The state

The Church's peaceableness also challenges Constantinianism or the control of the Church by the state. Hauerwas believes that Constantinianism reduces the Church to a department of the state and conflates baptism and citizenship. Consequently church membership requires no additional or challenging disciplines beyond the basic requirements of citizenship. The distinctiveness of discipleship is thereby diluted and the pragmatics of statecraft rapidly subvert the integrity of the Church.[24] This renders the Church invisible and disembodied, whereas the integrity of the Church requires a different politics, more akin to that known before Constantine and latterly exemplified in the minority Anabaptist tradition. Only by distinguishing itself from its surrounding society can the Church act as significant witness to the Kingdom of God and thereby fulfil its prophetic task.[25] There needs to be clear blue water between the Church and the world, both to display the character of living holiness and also to prevent the Church being tempted to rule with the weapons of the world by using violence, effectiveness and success to evaluate and achieve its ends. This temptation, Hauerwas believes, is present in some aspects of liberation theology as well as in more traditional state politics. Both countenance the use of non-Christian means to achieve their goals, thereby corrupting the character of the Christian community and its witness to the peaceable reign of God. In effect, they therefore underwrite and legitimate the violent agenda of the liberal state. Constantinianism changed the character of Christian mission by rendering it a mission of imposition and violence rather than of peaceable sharing and attraction. In contrast, Christians need to develop the virtue of patience and the skills of tactical resistance to Constantinian mission, aware that though they cannot make liberal societies peaceable, they can witness as peaceable gestures to God's mission within such societies.[26]

Power

Peaceableness, though, is not powerless. Peaceableness itself is a form of power since it subverts coercive power in favour of friendship and the building up of community. In this way Christian relationships are characterized by trust rather than suspicion. In addition, the power of the Church is the power of the crucified, risen Jesus embodied within it. Thus his victory resources the Church's power for living holiness and illuminates the Church's understanding, for example, of medicine, marriage and the family. Not only does this Christian narrative of power deconstruct the pretensions of medical totalitarianism, as we saw in Chapter 2, but it reminds Christians that marriage and the biological family are secondary realities located within the primary reality of the Church and represent offices or callings within that fundamental vocation. In the Church, children are God's gifts to the whole community, rendering all Christians siblings and responsible parents. In addition, the character of Christian friendship means that all children are to be received as gifts, particularly those who are disabled. The latter represent the challenge of welcoming the stranger, which Jesus set as a critical indicator of discipleship. The Christian narrative of power expressed in the trusting and peaceable living of the Christian community is also a response to questions about theodicy. Theodicy presumes that human beings can survey the totality of reality and make judgements about God's activity within this. Christian living recognizes that this is impossible and that no human agent or community exists in such a relationship to reality. Instead, the Church trusts that Jesus' promise to be with the Church to the end of the age ensures that the truth about God's working is found not by speculation but through faithful worship. This worship is tested by its willingness to embrace the marginal and 'abnormal' in ways that embody the peaceable love of God.

The Church's habits

The formation of Christian habits which train Christians in the virtues necessary to perform their faith in ways faithful to the gospel is vital for the mission of the Church.[27] Hauerwas uses the confrontation between Henry VIII and Sir Thomas More as an example of the effects of such formation, since Thomas cannot but resist Henry because he is formed to see his loyalty to the monarch through his primary loyalty to God. Similarly, Olin Teague, a Mennonite businessman, cannot sue in a legal case because his Church has formed in him the habits of discipleship exemplified in 1 Corinthians 6.1–8.[28] Christian habits such as welcoming the stranger, visiting the sick, caring for the vulnerable and the like, generate a distinctive approach to medicine. These protect the Christian medic from being colonized by an instrumental and utilitarian view of medicine that sees cure as all and abnormality as a problem to be removed. They also help the Christian to survive faithfully within a society hostile to their way of life. Like peasants without much formal power, Christians are to practise their discipleship with patience and with each other so that they can learn when to resist the state's encroaching and when they can tactically co-operate. Given the particulars of their situations, such tactics will not be clearly evident in advance, but will become apparent through contextual discernment rooted in the formation of these habits.[29] Consequently these habits are the powers that make Christians human and are most apparent in the lives of the Church's saints and martyrs.[30] The saints and martyrs embody and exhibit the pattern and shape of ordinary Christian living in a more intense way. In addition, as the story of Thomas More displays, the way they lived and died denies their killers the power of determining the meaning of their existence. This can only be properly given through the Christian story within which they represent examples of those who lived and died trusting that human destiny is secure in the hands of God. As Hauerwas comments, 'Christians are not called to be heroes or shoppers. We are called to be holy.'[31]

The Church's hospitality

The Church is to live in a manner relevant to Christ rather than to the agenda of those who do not yet worship the true God as a prophetic sign of God's presence and ways in the world. This does not mean that the Church isolates itself from others. Rather, just as Jesus welcomes the stranger and seeks to befriend his enemies, so the Church is to be a hospitable community befriending those who are beyond it and different from it. Thus, as Wannenwetsch comments, the Church is to be a trusting community rather than a community of suspicion.[32] Friendship is a particularly definitive practice for the Church in this regard because it respects the other person in a non-manipulative manner and thereby bears witness to the grace of God. In addition, it depends upon truth-telling if it is to be genuine friendship and challenges self-deception by such truthful speaking. Furthermore, the Church is not threatened by the stranger, since as sinners they have discovered God's forgiveness through the practices of reconciliation, such as confession, forgiveness and absolution. They are therefore no longer strangers but friends of God whose witness entails befriending other strangers and orientating them to this divine friendship. Thus an inner urban church refusing to desert a challenging area and offering an open Sunday meal to its neighbourhood as a continuation of the Eucharist symbolizes the tenacity of Christian friendship and hospitality.

Such a disposition to friendship and care for the stranger has particular force in late modern societies captivated as they are by the cults of celebrity and expertise. These inevitably diminish the significance of ordinary people and marginalize those who, through appearance, ability or opportunity, cannot access these places of power. Hauerwas holds that the catholicity of the Church is indicated by the presence within it of those whom the world rejects or ignores. In addition, these folk protect the Church from self-preoccupation and self-interest as they demand attention and time. They also save the Church from the temptation to mystify the gospel and promote a disembodied faith because they locate people rather than abstract ideals or notions of normality at the heart of the Church. Indeed, if the Church becomes a community which excludes such people, it ceases to reflect the universal grace of God and becomes akin to a liberal sect.

The Church's worship[33]

Worshipping with ordinary Christians in ordinary churches, therefore, takes on a new vitality, since it is here that people are appropriately formed to embody the faith, live in God's time and represent, thereby, a faithful witness.[34] 'Worship is the practice that sums up or gives direction to all we do as Christians. It is the fundamental performance of faith that, for example, shapes what we talk about and how we talk as Christians.'[35] Here, too, in contrast to modernity, freedom and truth are in communion since liturgy directs attention to God rather than reinforcing self-love. Freedom is now for God and others rather than for the self. Truth is discovered with God and others rather than alone.[36] Thus, instead of simply being a reservoir from which Christian activists or clerical candidates are sourced, the local congregation is a theological agency of irreplaceable value. It is a 'base community' witnessing in its particularity to the universal grace of God. This in part explains why Hauerwas is ambivalent about the professionalization of theology, which he calls 'a Babylonian captivity of theology by the Enlightenment university'.[37] It is also why he has taken to teaching Christian ethics through liturgy, since 'the formation of Christians through the liturgy makes clear that Christians are not simply called to do the "right thing", but rather we are expected to be holy'.[38] Being gathered to worship properly acts as a sign of the politics and ethics of God as Christians are both identified and formed into witnesses of Christ who are taught how to name God. Through confession and listening to Scripture they are enabled to recognize sin and locate themselves in the story of God. Eucharist speaks of God's sacrifice for the world within which Christians are included and puts an end to all other sacrifices, such as capital punishment and war. The dismissal sends Christians into the world to witness and serve self-consciously as Christians rather than simply citizens employing the discriminatory skills which worship has given them.[39]

In the light of this, Hauerwas is clear that Christian theologians are to assist the Church in its way of life rather than preoccupy themselves with academic speculation. 'God does not redeem us in the abstract, but as people who are constituted in and by concrete histories.'[40] This contrasts with the ethos of contemporary universities within which many Christian theologians are located. He believes that the university has been colonized by the disembodied unaccountable individualism of the modern world with its instrumental and calculative approach to reality. The effect of this has been to mutate Christianity into a set of beliefs that can be disconnected from the practices of the Church. He sees this abstract faith as a new form of Gnosticism, a belief which has no requirement for the materiality which Christ's incarnation reveals to be at the heart of Christianity.[41] This divinely infused materiality is expressed in the gathered congregation and makes the interpretation of the Church a fundamental task for theologians. In consequence, Christian theologians need to go to church, since it is here that the intensities of Christian character are exposed and the ongoing story of Jesus is embodied across the diversities of culture, time and geography.[42]

Conclusion

Hauerwas's commitment to embodied holiness expressed in the peaceable living of the Christian community restores to the Church a distinctive witness in late modern societies. It suggests what we might expect to see as Christians worship God and are transformed thereby into iconic communities of faith. We would expect to see:

- Communities characterized by practical ways of expressing the peaceable character of Christ, particularly among the violent and estranged.

- A very material and fleshly spirituality expressed in corporate worship, a distinctively Christian way of living and tangible service to the world.
- Churches as communities with a common life rather than as voluntary collections of individuals gathering to foster their own interests.
- Communities whose agenda is set by God in worship rather than by the mores of contemporary society or the power of the state. These communities would actively engage with and serve these societies, but their service would be accountable to the divine story rather than the demands of those in power.
- Communities committed to remembering and living out of the past rather than seeking to escape from that past. They would be consciously aware of their narrative and therefore historical identity.
- Communities free from anxiety about their own survival and confident in the vocation God has given them as contemporary witnesses to Christ. This would be expressed in their care for those whom the world has no time or patience for.
- Communities committed to fostering those habits of life which generate the critical Christian virtues of peacemaking, friendship, trust and hospitality.
- An international and inter-generational community of Christian communities who consciously seek to live in conversation with their eschatological destiny and their history.

Such a series of expectations inevitably raises many questions and criticisms, some of which we will explore in the next chapter. However, though they can be posed, they do not allow us to avoid the formidable challenge that Hauerwas presents to the contemporary Church.

Questions

- What do you think about Hauerwas's view of the Church's politics?
- How might your church help Christians learn better habits?
- What does Hauerwas's work imply about the international Church?
- How does Hauerwas's project help you engage with the particular challenges of living in a late modern society?

Further reading

Bartley, Jonathan, *Faith and Politics After Christendom: The Church as a Movement for Anarchy*, Milton Keynes: Paternoster, 2006.

Giddens, Anthony, *Modernity and Self-Identity: Self and Society in the Late Modern Age*, Cambridge: Polity Press, 1991.

Hauerwas, Stanley, *Sanctify Them in the Truth: Holiness Exemplified*, Edinburgh: T. & T. Clark, 1998.

—— *A Better Hope: Resources for a Church Confronting Capitalism, Democracy and Postmodernity*, Grand Rapids: Brazos Press, 2000.

—— *Performing the Faith: Bonhoeffer and the Practice of Nonviolence*, London: SPCK, 2004.

Ramsey, Paul, *War and the Christian Conscience: How Shall Modern War be Conducted Justly?*, 4th edn, Durham: Duke University Press, 1976.

Rasmusson, Arne, *The Church as Polis: From Political Theology to Theological Politics as Exemplified by Jürgen Moltmann and Stanley Hauerwas*, Notre Dame: University of Notre Dame Press, 1995.

Thomson, John B., *The Ecclesiology of Stanley Hauerwas*, Aldershot: Ashgate, 2003.

Notes

1 *Performing the Faith: Bonhoeffer and the Practice of Nonviolence*, London: SPCK, 2004, p. 19.

2 *With the Grain of the Universe: The Church, Witness and Natural Theology*, Grand Rapids: Brazos Press, 2001, p. 216.

3 *Sanctify Them in the Truth: Holiness Exemplified*, Edinburgh: T. & T. Clark, 1998, p. 78.

4 *Sanctify Them*, p. 78.

5 *Sanctify Them*, pp. 77–90 and 101.

6 *A Better Hope: Resources for a Church Confronting Capitalism, Democracy and Postmodernity*, Grand Rapids: Brazos Press, 2000, p. 17.

7 *In Good Company: The Church as Polis*, Notre Dame: University of Notre Dame Press, 1995, pp. 67–8, 73, and *With the Grain of the Universe*, p. 14.

8 *A Better Hope*, pp. 9–10.

9 *A Better Hope*, p. 18.

10 *Wilderness Wanderings: Probing Twentieth-Century Theology and Philosophy*, Boulder: Westview Press, 1997, pp. 48–62 and *A Better Hope*, p. 25.

11 Arne Rasmusson, *The Church as Polis: From Political Theology to Theological Politics as Exemplified by Jürgen Moltmann and Stanley Hauerwas*, Notre Dame: University of Notre Dame Press, 1995.

12 *With the Grain*, pp. 217–18.

13 *In Good Company*, pp. 153–64.

14 *A Better Hope*, pp. 30–2, 139–54.

15 *Performing the Faith*, p. 39.

16 *A Better Hope*, p. 10.

17 *Sanctify Them*, pp. 177–89.

18 *Performing the Faith*, p. 15.

19 *Against the Nations: War and Survival in a Liberal Society*, Notre Dame: University of Notre Dame Press, 1992, pp. 132, 163, *Dispatches from the Front: Theological Engagements with the Secular*, Durham and London: Duke University Press, 1994, p. 125, and Stanley Hauerwas, Chris K. Heubner, Harry J. Heubner and Mark Thiessen Nation, *The Wisdom of the Cross: Essays in Honor of John Howard Yoder*, Grand Rapids: Eerdmans, 1999, p. 402.

20 *Dispatches from the Front*, pp. 117–50.

21 *A Better Hope*, pp. 173–88.

22 Stanley Hauerwas, 'Many Hands Working: A Response to Charles Mathewes', *Anglican Theological Review*, 82/2, 2000, 361–4, p. 362.

23 *Against the Nations*, p. 16.

24 *Christian Existence Today: Essays on Church, World and Living in Between*, Durham: The Labyrinth Press, 1988, pp. 171–90.

25 *Christian Existence Today*, p. 160.

26 *Sanctify Them*, pp 78–80.

27 *Performing the Faith*, pp. 156–9.

28 *Christian Existence Today*, pp. 74–85.

29 For Hauerwas's example of peasant patience and tactical engagement see *Christian Existence Today*, p. 13, *Dispatches from the Front*, pp. 104–5, and *Sanctify Them*, p. 75.

30 *Christian Existence Today*, p. 101, and *Sanctify Them*, pp. 123–42.

31 Stanley Hauerwas and Frank Lentricchia (eds), 'Dissent from the Homeland: Essays after September 11th', *South Atlantic Quarterly*, Spring 2002, p. 432.

32 Bernd Wannenwetsch, 'The Political Worship of the Church: A Critical and Empowering Practice', *Modern Theology*, 12/3, 1996, 268–94, p. 288.

33 The connection between the two is most explicit in the way Hauerwas and Wells have configured their work, *The Blackwell Companion to Christian Ethics*, which approaches ethics through the lens of liturgical worship. See Stanley Hauerwas and Samuel Wells, *The Blackwell Companion to Christian Ethics*, Oxford: Blackwell, 2006.

34 *Performing the Faith*, pp. 96–100, 152–69.

35 *A Better Hope*, p. 19.

36 *A Better Hope*, pp. 15–16.

37 'The Testament of Friends', *The Christian Century*, 107/7, 28 February 1990, 212–16, p. 215, and *Sanctify Them*, p. 6, footnote 10.

38 *In Good Company*, p. 155.

39 *In Good Company*, pp. 153–63.

40 'A Response to Quinn: Athens May Be a Long Way From Jerusalem But Prussia Is Even Further', *Asbury Theological Journal*, 45/1, Spring 1990, 59–64, p. 60.

41 *The State of the University: Academic Knowledge and the Knowledge of God*, Oxford: Blackwell, 2007, pp, 37, 51–2.

42 *In Good Company*, p. 11.

4

Challenging Holiness

Hauerwas engages the Church in a rich conversation about its worship, ethics, character, virtues, story, practices, performance, politics and witness. Inevitably the nature of his work has attracted criticisms. While I cannot deal with all of these, I will discuss the most important in this chapter. To help the reader engage with these criticisms I shall first clarify the challenges, then suggest how Hauerwas responds to them, and finally offer my own viewpoint on the question. At the end of each section I will provide questions for reflection in the boxes.

'Hauerwas cuts the Church off from wider society'

A number of critics have charged Hauerwas with fideism, tribalism, sectarianism and social withdrawal, which are all related to his focus upon the Church as the primary community for Christians.[1]

Hauerwas

'Fideism' is a term used to describe views based solely on faith or belief without any foundation in reason or empirical evidence. Hauerwas, like many thinkers today, does not believe that there is any agreed or singular foundation in reason or empirical evidence for human knowing.[2] All human knowing has elements of faith or belief present in its assumptions, so it is unfair to use this as a basis to dismiss his claims to a truthful way of speaking about God and the world.

Tribalism is a way of suggesting that Hauerwas's ideas relate only to fellow Christians and that those who are not part of the Church cannot understand them. Yet while his focus is firstly upon the Church, this does not mean that what he describes is limited to a small constituency of people. Certainly tribalism may help the Church to be aware of its particularity and defend it against the homogenizing singularity of liberal societies.[3] But as we noted in previous chapters, he challenges his critics by pointing out that the catholicity of the Church, through time and across the globe, is a sign of the universal appeal of Christianity. Christianity has shown its capacity historically and globally to engage people of all backgrounds. Indeed, this community is much more universal than the more limited world of his critics, rooted as they are in the minority North Atlantic tradition of thought.

Sectarianism is a way of suggesting that Hauerwas's thinking divides rather than bridges gaps between people. It implies that he is only interested in the Church and has no concern for wider society. However, Hauerwas challenges the vantage point of his critics. Given its historical and contemporary reach, the Church is a less sectarian community than the more limited world of his North Atlantic critics. In addition, given the absence of any universal vantage point from which to see or understand everything, all human thinking necessarily takes place within communities and contexts. The question is not about whether Hauerwas is especially sectarian but about how any human thinking, rooted as it is within the limitations of time, community and place, can escape being sectarian. As we saw in the preceding chapters, his work on truth, narrative, catholicity and the politics of the Church suggests that his project offers a less sectarian approach than his critics.

The charge of social withdrawal relates to Hauerwas's belief that the Church is the primary community of the Christian. However, he does not want Christians to withdraw from engaging with those beyond the Church. Rather, he wants Christians to engage self-consciously as Christians.[4] His principal concern is that when Christians engage with the world, they tend either to hide their convictions or feel that they must be relevant to the agendas of those outside the Church. Yet the Church should be relevant to the reign of God embodied in Christ rather than being uncritically enthralled to contemporary society. Consequently Christians will need to be clear about their basic identity as disciples of Jesus Christ if they are to engage with the world as Christians.

Viewpoint

These criticisms seem unfair to Hauerwas and are based on insecure assumptions. The presence of a community as extensive and diverse as the Church cannot easily be seen as sectarian, tribal or unengaged with those around it. Faith is certainly central to Christians, but this faith has a shape that can be seen. As we have been arguing, Hauerwas regards Christianity as a way of living which is about holiness embodied in flesh and blood. It is not primarily a set of ideas but is fundamentally a way of living together as the Church in God's world reaching out to others with the challenging friendship of God.

Questions

- How successful do you think Hauerwas is in resisting his critics?
- What does his defence help you to appreciate about being part of the Church?
- In what ways might the history of the Church subvert Hauerwas's defence?

The meaning and impact of Constantinianism

As mentioned in Chapter 1, Constantinianism is a way of describing the relationship between Church and society after the conversion in the early fourth century of the Roman Emperor Constantine. This ended three centuries of persecution as the empire became a nominally Christian society governed by two authorities, the one clerical and the other lay. The clergy's authority was formally rooted in the liturgical practices of the faith, and their role was to bring the community publicly to worship God. The emperor and subsequent leaders were authorities in the political life of the community charged to lead society through the lens of their devotional formation.

Hauerwas

As we have seen in earlier chapters, Hauerwas holds that the Constantinian pact subverted the peaceable holiness of the Church as the Church succumbed to the temptations of power and violence. Indeed, in his view it effectively became a department of state for much of history. Baptism and citizenship were equated so that the distinctive ethic of peaceable discipleship disappeared for most Christians. Such an approach has led to the invisibility of the Church in both Europe and America, even though American churchgoing remains reasonably robust. This is because in both contexts people can no longer distinguish between being a good American or European citizen and being a Christian.[5] Consequently the churches have nothing with which to challenge such societies, nor are they able to hold their own members to any distinctive way of life.[6] In this Hauerwas follows the thought of John Howard Yoder and the Anabaptist tradition, as we saw in Chapter 3.

Viewpoint

Yet in advocating this Anabaptist critique, Hauerwas misunderstands Constantinianism. In European history the religious settlement which Hauerwas calls Constantinianism was and remains a contingent expression of a Christian society whose rulers claim to be disciples.[7] Historically it was not about the Church being subservient to the state but rather about the state accepting its place within the Church such that 'temporal and spiritual affairs are two separate functions of one and the same community'.[8] The emperor upon conversion became part of the Church and this inevitably set up new challenges which earlier Christians had not had to face. In the short run it was seen by protagonists such as Eusebius of Caesarea as the inauguration of the millennial era of peace, since the whole known world was now in public submission to Christ. In this regard he was mistaken, but the significance of the empire formally submitting its life to the disciplines of the Church should not be underestimated nor seen as necessarily antagonistic to Christian witness and mission. Those who present themselves for baptism are welcomed and then inducted into the practices of discipleship, whether they be the emperor or anyone else. Indeed, in some way the religious settlement in Europe was formally the obverse of this construal of Constantinianism, since it involved the emperor or secular power accepting the disciplines of Christian discipleship mediated through worship. Of course, Hauerwas is correct to question the actual cost of this approach to the faithful witness of the Church, since it was often subverted by the secular powers and indeed by the clergy, as was evident during the Investiture Dispute and the Reformation. However, while hindsight enables us to criticize much that emerged from this concord, it does not follow that it was intrinsically wrong given Constantine's request for baptism.

Sadly, throughout the history of the Church there are numerous examples of the problematic relationship between these two dimensions of a Christian society, such as Constantine's role in the fourth-century Arian controversy or the Papacy's lofty political ambitions in the medieval Investiture Disputes. Yet, although there have been abuses of power by both spiritual and temporal authorities, these do not undermine this aspiration for a Christian society nor imply its intrinsic violence. Indeed, Constantinianism still reflects the formal relationship between the spiritual and temporal authorities in much of Europe. Furthermore, there is historical evidence that Constantinianism did not necessarily imply a crusading approach to difference, for example in the conversations between medieval Islam and Christianity represented by Christian theologians such as Albert the Great and Thomas Aquinas and Muslim thinkers such as Averoes and Avicenna.

In addition, it could be argued that the attempt by the United

States to segregate the spiritual and temporal within the public square has actually rendered American society more secular than its European counterparts even though churchgoing in the United States remains much higher.[9] Consequently, despite seeming more secular, contemporary politics in Europe are actually more indebted to and bound up with their Christian roots than those of the United States. For example, the Church of England still remains the church of first resort for most of the majority Christian community in England, and is able to offer catholic pastoral care through its parishes without this appearing imperialistic. Its relatively small congregational base does not reflect its significance in a society where participation in anything perceived as voluntary is minimal. Indeed, the way Christianity is embodied in England means that its embedded character enables small communities and their clergy to engage with all sorts of people across the social spectrum in remarkable ways. In so doing they represent a provisional and faithful sign of the Kingdom of God rather than the fullness of that kingdom.[10]

Questions

- How convincing do you find Hauerwas's concerns about Constantinianism?
- Can you think of ways in which Church and state/society need to re-imagine their relationship today in the light of Hauerwas's challenges?

Holiness and eschatology

The third challenge questions Hauerwas's understanding of the relationship between God's future or eschatology and the contemporary life of the Church. Eschatology is that dimension of theology which deals with the final destiny of creation, and Hauerwas argues that this destiny is to be realized in contemporary Church witness rather than simply hoped for in the future.

Hauerwas

Hauerwas believes the Church should live eschatologically, or in the light of its divinely ordained destiny, which he believes to be the universal peace of God exemplified in the life and Passion of Jesus Christ. He sees in Christ's life, death and resurrection not simply the singular path of a unique historical individual but the ongoing calling of the Church as the body of Christ to be a wholly non-violent community. Peaceableness is not motivated by the desire to survive but by the imperative to be faithful, since such survivalism involves human self-preoccupation rather than a trusting witness to God's providence. Hauerwas regards the way of non-violence embodied by Christ and lived by Christians, Christ's contemporary body, to be the distinctive identity mark of the Church.[11] It is what he calls the epistemological key to the Church.[12] Peaceableness is the vocation of all Christians and through its divine validation in Christ is about living eschatologically with the grain of the universe, however surprising that may seem.

Viewpoint

Hauerwas's peaceable kingdom trades on the eschatology of John Howard Yoder which itself depends upon interpreting the life, death and resurrection of Jesus as the pattern or way for contemporary Christian social practice. Yet such an interpretation effectively bypasses the history of most of the Church and underplays the latter's revelatory value despite Hauerwas's conviction that the life of the Church is the social life of Jesus through time. Furthermore, Yoder's eschatology conflates the variety of eschatologies present in the New Testament in order to form a single interpretative key for Christ and the Church's life.[13] Most historians and biblical scholars will testify to the problems attached to this sort of enterprise, since as contemporary interpreters our access to the past is mediated and complex.[14] Indeed, Hauerwas is himself aware of these problems and so locates the meaning of Jesus in the practices of the Church rather than in abstract interpretations of the past. We discover the way of Jesus for today as we live in the way of the Lord as Jesus and

Israel did. Yet, as Jeffrey Stout questions, 'Where are we to find the community of non-violent discipleship he has in mind?'[15] While Hauerwas's critique of Reinhold Niebuhr, Paul Ramsey and others has force, it is the falsifying practices of the majority Church that remain a challenge to the view that the Church is to recapitulate the particular vocation of Christ in the contemporary world and thereby to realize eschatology. In particular, his attempt to render Bonhoeffer an ally for his peaceable agenda leaves the latter's participation in the plot to assassinate Hitler unresolved, as Hauerwas himself admits.[16] It is clear that Bonhoeffer saw in peaceableness the condition for a truthful society. However, inhabiting one which was structured around such destructive lies as Nazism, forced a decision and action whose meaning remains uncertain.

So the challenge Reinhold Niebuhr wrestled with remains. Does the fallen and finite character of the world that God has not yet brought to glory and the history of the Church question the sort of radical peaceableness Hauerwas envisages? Has Hauerwas conflated the arrival of the Kingdom in Christ with the anticipated arrival of the Kingdom of glory mentioned by Paul in 1 Corinthians 15.24? If so, would this anachronistically expect of the Church a way of life appropriate to the fullness of that age rather than approximating to its first fruits?[17] It would equate the present body of Christ with the ascended glorified body of Christ. Yet the fallible performance of the Church through time questions whether the two are yet identical. The Second Advent implies something more than simply a removal of the veil of the Church's identity. In addition, if the Church infused by the Spirit is the first fruits of the kingdom it is on the way to glory rather than representing the fullness of that glory. In consequence, the way the majority of the Church has wrestled with issues of peaceable living should be seen as indicative of the action of the Spirit in the Church through time rather than evidence of the Church's unfaithfulness.[18] The Spirit in the Church through time illuminating the Scriptures and the tradition suggests a more approximate approach to peaceableness. Christians seek for the most peaceable possibility but recognize that in a world awaiting transformation into glory, such peaceableness is never absolute. This seems to be the issue that Bonhoeffer wrestled with and concluded in a similar way.

This quest for approximate peaceableness assumes a more elusive role for the Holy Spirit and challenges the attempt by Hauerwas to trace a definitive Christ-shaped life in the Church. It may offer a more fruitful way of acknowledging the provisionality and possibility of being the Church in the world as a fallible sign of the Kingdom of God. Christ's vocation was unique, and rather than replicating his vocation, the Church is called to follow him in the Spirit as the contemporary crucified and ascended Lord. The Scriptures and sacramental practices of the Church infused by the Spirit therefore engender diverse and contextually sensitive expressions of Christian living. While these are accountable to the witness of the Church through time, there may be occasions where they are not easily recognized by all Christians, particularly if they involve force or apparent violence. The just-war theory has many limitations, but it does represent an attempt to guide Christians in very difficult situations.

Although Hauerwas regards peaceableness, interpreted as non-violence, to be an essential indicator of the Church, this does not imply that those who cannot agree with such a precise equation are unable to appropriate other key insights of his project. For example, his attention to performance and practices suggests that the way Christians discover the call of God is by reflection upon such temporal practices. This means that Christians cannot know the particular way they are to live in advance or in the abstract. The past and the stories of Christ offer bearings, but they do not control the future.

Questions

- If Hauerwas is correct about the Church's peaceable vocation, what would this imply for today's Church?
- What sort of counsel should the Church be giving Christians in the armed forces or in the police forces?

Holiness and practices

A further challenge to Hauerwas's thinking is made by Christopher Insole. He questions Hauerwas's appropriation of the philosopher Ludwig Wittgenstein's views on the relationship between truth, meaning and the practices of the Church.[19] According to Insole, Wittgenstein claims that meaning is a function of the use of language within the context of particular shared practices and forms of life. To know what a concept means, we need to know how it is used in such 'practices'. This claim can be interpreted in two possible ways. In the first interpretation, practices are seen as the social activities of actual communities which are community specific and that the truth and meaning of these practices are what this community intends. These are therefore inaccessible to those not yet inducted into the community's interpretation of the practice. They function as a consensual, communal and thereby constructive view of language which is effectively secret. The second interpretation is that practices are social activities that enable us to progress through life in a way that can be communicated to others and are therefore publicly intelligible. For Insole, the first interpretation makes scepticism impossible, renders the truth claims of different practices incommensurable and ensures that proponents appear separatist and arrogant. The second interpretation leaves open the possibility that truth transcends a particular community, making possible more open and eirenic approaches to other truth-claiming practices. We grasp truth because we are human rather than because we are churched.

Insole argues that the first interpretation was not held by Wittgenstein, though it is attractive to some who employ his thought. Insole believes that one of these may be Hauerwas. He is concerned that Hauerwas presents practices not simply as manifestations of beliefs but as constitutive of those beliefs. Yet paradoxically, Hauerwas's use of the unbeliever Wittgenstein as an ally actually indicates the communicability of truth beyond a particular community and undermines any notion of a community-determined meaning for practices. In addition, according to Insole, Hauerwas underplays the diversity of practices present within the churches that make the latter's case for common Christian truth less plausible. Furthermore, Insole believes that Hauerwas's communal, consensual notion of practices depends upon the sort of realized eschatology and a triumphalist, sectarian view of the Church that we have discussed above. This sits ill with the ambiguous stories of discipleship in the biblical texts and is actually very secularist, since it is very sceptical about what the Enlightenment project can deliver and therefore seeks to distance itself from the latter. Insole certainly recognizes that Hauerwas speaks of the Christian imperative to befriend the stranger, to be open to those outside the Church and to regard the Kingdom of God as broader than the Church. However, he sees this as a contradictory and reactionary response to the logic of his fundamental position. In addition, it is also unbiblical since it assumes that the Church can distinguish between the outsider and the insider rather than having such distinctions subverted, as often happens in the New Testament stories. These subversive stories suggest that God is not locked into our practices but surprises us from beyond and in the outsider. Insole also wonders whether Wittgenstein is a helpful ally for Hauerwas, given his view that theological meaning is wholly immanent to Christian practice. In contrast, Insole believes that religious practices include the notion that divine truth is not simply identical with them though it is identified with them. Truth transcends practices. The Christian community does not have authorial control over the reception of their texts.

Hauerwas

Insole's critique of Hauerwas's use of Wittgenstein is a powerful one and identifies ambiguities in Hauerwas. Yet Hauerwas himself argues that 'I certainly do not believe, nor did Wittgenstein, that religious convictions are or should be treated as an internally consistent language game that is self-validating.'[20] Furthermore, as Insole himself recognizes, it is behaviour rather than simply rhetoric which indicates the meaning of words/beliefs. It is therefore worth noting that Hauerwas started attending church as he grasped the character of Christian discipleship, and that he also belonged to churches located in inner urban areas such as Aldersgate Methodist or Broadway Methodist. Here he engaged with the estranged and experienced the challenge of relating to the outsider. In addition, he has been very public in his commitments to practical peaceableness, and his popular writing is premised on the capacity of his work to communicate beyond the Church. Hauerwas also advocates the importance of friendship in discerning the truth of God, friends who include Jews and Muslims as well as fellow Christians, and asserts that his work is about engaging with God rather than simply about the formation of a community.[21] Furthermore, *Wilderness Wanderings*, *Sanctify Them* and *With the Grain of the Universe* engage with the presence of God beyond the Church. Indeed, as he says, 'God's dominion is not limited or confined to the church … rather … its "origin", its most concentrated expression is there displayed.' For Hauerwas, the Church's politics expose the character of God's rule in nature.[22] Hence, participating in ecclesial practices attunes Christians to discern God's reign in the world.[23] Hauerwas accepts that conversations beyond the Church are challenging but this does not make them impossible. The Church is not a closed language.[24] Indeed, the Church is to be a Church for the world.[25]

Viewpoint

Hauerwas's concern throughout his work is to demonstrate the formative significance of discipleship practices as the means of understanding the Christian calling and thereby avoiding being at the mercy of other alien agendas. He rejects the notion that there is only one way of understanding the world and instead believes that different communities interpret the world in distinctive ways analogous to the way languages function.[26] Consequently, the truthfulness of these languages is not established by bringing them to the bar of a singular, universal perspective but by exploring their explanatory and illuminative capacity and by seeing what sort of people they form. Similarly, people can learn and understand second and third languages. Thus, by putting his thoughts in the public domain, Hauerwas accepts the porous character of community languages. Furthermore, the way Christian practices have engaged people across history and the world underwrites the Christian claim that the practices are infused with divine life, since the universal embrace of God is witnessed to in the sign of a Church of all peoples. He does not believe that his work is simply sociology rather than theology and regularly reminds readers of Christ's promise in the Eucharist to be with his people when his people gather.

Questions

- Why do you think Hauerwas believes the Church's practices matter so much?
- What would be the effect upon Hauerwas's project if Insole's criticisms were persuasive?

Holiness and the Church

A further challenge concerns both the fallibility of the Church and the historical ambiguity of reformism within the Church. As we noted above, Jeffrey Stout asks whether there has ever been a Church such as Hauerwas's, while Charles Taylor, in his most recent book *A Secular Age*, argues that reformist approaches, akin to Hauerwas's have actually contributed to secularization by dividing the holy from the profane in too rigorous a fashion.[27] In addition, Duncan Forrester points out the failure of the German Church to embody its story outside the Dachau camp even though there were noble examples of Christians of character within Dachau. This raises questions about whether Hauerwas should change his indicative tense to an imperative one when speaking of the Church.[28]

Hauerwas

Hauerwas regards sanctification, or how human beings become holy, as the effect of God's work in the Church rather than what the Church seeks to become for God. Although he expects this holiness to generate a peaceable way of living, this does not imply that a fallible Church is intrinsically unable to witness to the presence of grace in its life and in the world. It simply recognizes that transformation takes time and is often patchy and slow. As he says in response to Forrester, the Church as a social ethic is not a status but a task.[29] What he shows us is that the Christian story, mediated through the practices of attentive discipleship, has the resources within itself to critique its own abuses and also to listen to criticisms from without, since it is called to befriend even its enemies. Once again he is convinced that Christ's refusal to be absent from his people guarantees that they are being transformed, albeit on God's terms and in God's good time. If such sanctification contributes to a sharper distinction between the Church and the world, then Hauerwas simply sees this as both inevitable and beneficial for the world. The Church is not primarily concerned with human flourishing but rather with human transformation. It is only as such a distinction happens that the world can be given its story and the character of the gospel illustrated persuasively.

Viewpoint

Hauerwas may be over-confident in the peaceable possibilities of the Church, but his emphasis on God as the agent who renders the Church a faithful witness acts as an important counter to human-centred views of sanctification. In addition, there is the cumulative effect of God's grace upon the lives of those open to that grace which generates a significant, though not exhaustive, sign of God's life within them.[30] Certainly, co-operation and confession are integral to this relationship. However, the effectiveness of the Church's living holiness resides in the activity of God within it and is guaranteed by the risen, ascended Christ's refusal to divorce himself from this community. This responds to Charles Taylor's concerns, since if the Church is faithful it will inevitably become a contrast to the world and thereby witness to the gospel truthfully. To subvert or diminish this distinctiveness subverts and diminishes the gospel. Yet, as we have also seen, Hauerwas stresses friendship as intrinsic to Christian practice and so this distinctiveness is not necessarily sectarian or tribalist. It is rather about the Church being a sign to the world of God's invitation to all to become part of Jesus' universal community.

Questions

- What do you feel about Hauerwas's stress on the agency of God in sanctification?
- In what ways does the fallibility of the Church aid the witness of the Church?
- How can the Church be both distinctive and hospitable to those not yet part of it?

Church and creation

Another challenge posed to Hauerwas is that his theological politics is too human-centred and neglectful of important and pressing ecological issues. Consequently, do his concerns about Church, language and sociality need to be complemented by more work on the relationship between the Church and creation?

Hauerwas

It is true that Hauerwas does not engage substantively with ecological issues.[31] Indeed, one of his most recent publications, *The Blackwell Companion to Christian Ethics*, has only one chapter explicitly dealing with this theme.[32] Yet, as he comments in his 1993 reflections on Pope John Paul's encyclical *Veritatis Splendor*, his commitment to the story of God witnessed to in Scripture and the performance of the Church through time involves an awareness of being created as part of God's world.[33] Indeed, without the Church, people would not realize that they were creatures at all or that creation is an environment of gift with correlative accountabilities.[34] Furthermore, his interest in vegetarianism as a witness to peaceableness and also the materiality of his spirituality indicate his sensitivity to creation.[35]

Viewpoint

Hauerwas could contribute more to the ecological debate, but it would be unfair to diminish the significance of his project simply because it does not attempt to deal with everything. In part, Hauerwas represents the contextual challenges of his time within the American Church and academy, an era which he believes has seriously compromised the Church's witness as such. Hauerwas believes that creation will not be recognized as God's creation without the distinctive and social witness of the Church. Ecological issues are seen in this light.

Questions

- What sort of approach do you think Hauerwas would take if he engaged more fully with ecological issues?
- How might Hauerwas's church politics be challenged by contemporary ecological concerns?

Theological rootedness

This charge is made by Professor Nigel Biggar, who asks whether Hauerwas's Church is necessarily rooted in the reality of God or whether it is simply a community using church language and practices to give itself a social shape and meaning in the world much akin to the way the sociologist Emil Durkheim understood the relationship between religion and society? [36]

Hauerwas

Hauerwas describes his work as properly theology or a reflection on relationship between God and the world. Nevertheless, in his view the first theological task is not to ask whether God exists, but whether we exist, and is not to make God intelligible to us but rather to make us intelligible to God. The social and historical reality of the Church expresses the universality of God as one who draws all peoples into the Kingdom.[37] Indeed, Biggar himself recognizes the way the centrality of eschatology and of the Church as witness to God's redeeming of the world in Hauerwas's thinking counters the view that his Church is a Durkheimian religious sect.[38] Rather, this universal hospitality renders the Church necessarily open to truth wherever it is being discovered.[39] Theology is consequently about following the grain of the universe by living faithfully before and with this God.[40] However, the historic ambiguity of the Church's tradition does raise significant challenges to substantial ecclesial politics.[41] Indeed, the western tradition can be seen as an attempt to respond to this ambiguous legacy evident in the medieval Investiture Dispute, the divine right of kings ideology, the godly republic of Cromwell and the sixteenth- and seventeenth-century wars of religion.

Viewpoint

Hauerwas roots his understanding of the Church in theology. The Church is not simply a sociological construction but a divine society. In addition, his work on formation indicates why Christian theologians need to participate in the Church if they are to do theology properly. As a result, Hauerwas has also recovered the theological significance of the local congregation. The presence of distinctive Christian communities formed by worship and discipleship practices to witness to and serve God in the world represent contextual embodied apologetics for the gospel. They provide the tangible resources for theological reflection.

Questions

- Why is it so important that Hauerwas's work is theology?
- What theological resources does your local church possess?
- How are North Atlantic societies still rooted in theology?

Intellectual coherence

Hauerwas's style, which involves writing ad hoc essays rather than a systematic treatise, has raised questions about whether his project has any coherence or whether it is simply postmodern anarchy.

Hauerwas

Hauerwas does not believe in finished theological systems. His theological approach involves asking questions evoked by the practices of the Church and its vocation in the world, which are necessarily contextual since they are raised within the limitations and dynamics of time, place and community. Thus, this is theology on the move and the essay and sermon formats exemplify this.

Viewpoint

Although Hauerwas prefers occasional essays to systematic books, his exploration of narrative and the way he gathers groups of essays thematically imply that his project has shape and coherence. Such shape is not a return to modernist ideas about abstract systematic thought rooted in a spectator view of knowledge. Rather, the shape is grasped retrospectively as he and we look back at his work and notice connections emerging as questions are asked and stories explored. In consequence, we can describe his project as a work in progress since this re-narrating of his project throws up the next questions to be responded to. In the process he finds fellow travellers, such as Aristotle, Thomas Aquinas, Karl Barth, George Lindbeck, John Howard Yoder and Alasdair MacIntyre, as well as thinkers he disagrees with such as Walter Rauschenbusch, Reinhold Niebuhr and Paul Ramsey. The way he relates his work to their work also indicates a sense of coherence represented in the very act of conversation. In all of this, Hauerwas shows us that it is in the activity of living rather than in abstract thought that a coherent understanding of the ways of God with the world can be found. Such living is itself given a shape through the formative experience of inhabiting the stories of faith mediated by the Church in its practices and performances. In this way, the Church once again is what gives Hauerwas's work its coherence.

Questions

- How does Hauerwas's essay style help the Church to do theology?
- Can you re-narrate Hauerwas's theological journey?
- How would you tell the story of your church's theological journey?

Conclusion

In this chapter I have explored a number of challenges to Hauerwas's project: fideism, tribalism, sectarianism, social withdrawal, his views on Constantinianism, eschatology, peaceableness, practices, sanctification, ecology and theology. While some have more force than others, I don't believe they undermine the fruitfulness of that project for the contemporary Church, particularly in its local expression. In the second part of this book I want to improvise upon aspects of his work using my own experience as a parish priest and now a diocesan officer. Such an approach is inevitably ad hoc and limited. However, I hope that it will encourage others to engage with Hauerwas's work in their own contexts.

Notes

1 Wilson D. Miscamble, 'Sectarian Passivism', and Michael J. Quirk, 'Beyond Sectarianism', together with Hauerwas's reply, 'Will the Real Sectarian Stand Up!', in *Theology Today*, 44/1, April 1987, pp. 70–94. See also his rejection of these charges as argued below in the introduction to *Christian Existence Today: Essays on Church, World and Living in Between*, Durham: The Labyrinth Press, 1988, pp. 4–18, and in *A Better Hope: Resources for a Church Confronting Capitalism, Democracy and Postmodernity*, Grand Rapids: Brazos Press, 2000, pp. 23–34.

2 Stanley Hauerwas, Nancy Murphy and Mark Nation (eds), *Theology Without Foundations: Religious Practice and the Future of Theological Truth*, Nashville: Abingdon Press, 1994.

3 Stanley Hauerwas, 'On the Right to be Tribal', *Christian Scholars Review*, 16/3, 1987, p. 241.

4 *In Good Company: The Church as Polis*, Notre Dame: University of Notre Dame Press, 1995, p. 1, and *A Better Hope*, p. 24.

5 *Christian Existence Today*, pp. 171–90.

6 *Christian Existence Today*, p. 160.

7 For an attempt to recover a plausible Constantinianism for today, see Oliver O'Donovan, *The Desire of Nations: Rediscovering the Roots of Political Theology*, Cambridge: Cambridge University Press, 1996.

8 Paul Avis, *Anglicanism and the Christian Church: Theological Resources in Historical Perspective*, Edinburgh: T. & T. Clark, 1989, p. 61.

9 See the work of Grace Davie, *Europe: The Exceptional Case: Parameters of Faith in the Modern World*, London: Darton, Longman & Todd, 2002, *The Sociology of Religion*, London: Sage, 2007, and Grace Davie, Paul Heelas and Linda Woodhead (eds), *Predicting Religion: Christian, Secular and Alternative Futures*, Aldershot: Ashgate, 2003. See also Oliver O'Donovan, *The Ways of Judgment*, Cambridge: Eerdmans, 2005.

10 For a different viewpoint from the one I advocate, see Jonathan Bartley, *Faith and Politics After Christendom: The Church as a Movement for Anarchy*, Milton Keynes: Paternoster, 2006.

11 *Christian Existence Today*, p. 1.

12 *Christian Existence Today*, p. 1.

13 See the comments of Thomas W. Ogletree, *The Use of the Bible in Christian Ethics*, Philadelphia: Fortress Press, 1987, p. 117.

14 Rowan Williams, *Why Study the Past? The Quest for the Historical Church*, London: Darton, Longman & Todd, 2005.

15 Jeffrey Stout, *Democracy and Tradition*, Princeton: Princeton University Press, 2004, p. 160.

16 *Performing the Faith: Bonhoeffer and the Practice of Nonviolence*, London: SPCK, 2004, pp. 34–69.

17 For a discussion on this distinction see Jürgen Moltmann, *The Coming of God: Christian Eschatology*, London: SCM, 1996, p. 104, and Richard Baukham (ed.), *God Will Be All in All: The Eschatology of Jürgen Moltmann*, Edinburgh: T. & T. Clark, 1999, p. 286.

18 See Jeffrey Stout's plea that Hauerwas see the world as a realm ordered and ruled by God and hence one in which we can find God. *Democracy and Tradition*, p. 154.

19 Christopher J. Insole, 'The Truth Behind Practices: Wittgenstein, Robinson Crusoe and Ecclesiology', *Studies in Christian Ethics*, 20.3, 2007, pp. 364–82.

20 *Christian Existence Today*, p. 10.

21 *Wilderness Wanderings: Probing Twentieth-Century Theology and Philosophy*, Boulder: Westview Press, 1997, pp. xii–xiii. The reaction to the charge that his work 'is nothing more than reproducing Durkheim, albeit with an ecclesiological twist' relates to a conversation with Nigel Biggar where this question was raised. See *Sanctify Them in the Truth: Holiness Exemplified*, Edinburgh: T. & T. Clark, 1998, p. 37. On listening to Muslims see also Mark Thiessen Nation and Samuel Wells (eds), *Faithfulness and Fortitude: In Conversation with the Theological Ethics of Stanley Hauerwas*, Edinburgh: T. & T. Clark, 2000, p. 323.

22 *Sanctify Them*, p. 45.

23 For Hauerwas, creation and nature mutually illuminate each other, as the formative practices of Christian devotion help us to see. *With the Grain of the Universe: The Church, Witness and Natural Theology*, Grand Rapids: Brazos Press, 2001, p. 21.

24 *Wilderness Wanderings*, p. 6.

25 *A Better Hope*, p. 157.

26 See George A. Lindbeck, *The Nature of Doctrine: Religion in a Postliberal Age*, Philadelphia: Westminster Press, 1984.

27 Charles Taylor, *A Secular Age*, Cambridge: Belknap Press, 2007.

28 *Faithfulness and Fortitude*, pp. 189–210.

29 *Faithfulness and Fortitude*, p. 326.

30 See Robin Gill in *Churchgoing and Christian Ethics*, Cambridge: Cambridge University Press, 1999.

31 However, on his approach to ecology see *In Good Company: The Church as Polis*, Notre Dame: University of Notre Dame Press, 1995, pp. 185–97. On natural theology see *With the Grain of the Universe*.

32 Ben Quash, 'Treasuring Creation', in Stanley Hauerwas and Samuel Wells (eds), *The Blackwell Companion to Christian Ethics*, Oxford: Blackwell, 2006, pp. 306–19.

33 Stanley Hauerwas, 'The Pope Puts Theology Back into Moral Theology', in *Studies in Christian Ethics*, 7.2, 1994, p. 17.

34 David Ford and Dennis Stamps (eds), *Essentials of Christian Community: For Daniel W. Hardy on his 65th Birthday*, Edinburgh: T. & T. Clark, 1996, p. 46, *In Good Company*, pp. 191–7, and *Sanctify Them*, pp. 13, 44–5.

35 William H. Willimon and Stanley Hauerwas, with Scott C. Sage, *Lord Teach Us: The Lord's Prayer and the Christian Life*, Nashville: Abingdon Press, 1996, pp. 50 and 76.

36 *Sanctify Them*, p. 37.

37 *Sanctify Them*, pp. 38–9.

38 *Faithfulness and Fortitude*, p. 145, footnote 20.

39 See Hauerwas's debate with Miscamble and Quirk in Wilson D. Miscamble, 'Sectarian Passivism', *Theology Today*, 44/1, April 1987, pp. 69–77, and Stanley Hauerwas, 'Will the Real Sectarian Stand Up!', *Theology Today*, 44/1, April 1987, pp. 87–94.

40 See *With the Grain of the Universe*.

41 See, for example, Gloria Albrecht's feminist challenge to Hauerwas in Gloria Albrecht, 'In Good Company: The Church as Polis: Article Review', *Scottish Journal of Theology*, 50/2, 1997, pp. 218–27, and Hauerwas's response in 'Failure of Communication or A Case of Uncomprehending Feminism', *Scottish Journal of Theology*, 50/2, 1997, pp. 228–39.

Part Two

Improvising with Stanley Hauerwas

5

Congregational Holiness[1]

Themes from Hauerwas's work which inform this chapter are drawn from the following collections: *Vision and Virtue: Essays in Christian Ethical Reflection*; *Truthfulness and Tragedy: Further Investigations into Christian Ethics*; *A Community of Character: Toward a Constructive Christian Social Ethic*; *The Peaceable Kingdom: A Primer in Christian Ethics*; *After Christendom?*; *In Good Company: The Church as Polis*; *Lord Teach Us: The Lord's Prayer and the Christian Life*; and *Sanctify Them in the Truth: Holiness Exemplified*.

In Part One of this book I have discussed Hauerwas's work. In Part Two I want to improvise on themes from his work in the areas of congregational witness, discipleship, ministry and mission. In this chapter I tell the story of the inner urban congregation of St Mary's, Doncaster, where I was minister for eight years in the 1990s, in order to show how this Christian community offered a fragile yet distinctive witness to the grace of God. This story is not an abstract example or model of congregational performance, but is told to illustrate how the practices of common worship, hospitality, remembering and pastoral mission formed this particular community into a tangible witness to the transforming holiness of God. In order to do this, I will first describe the parish and its congregation. Then I will show how my engagement with Stanley Hauerwas's project illuminated the significance of such congregational witness. Finally I will tell the story of St Mary's to show how its witness emerged from a way of discipleship which itself tangibly spoke of God's activity in the world.

Living contextual holiness

During my time as incumbent, the parish of St Mary's, Wheatley in Doncaster was an inner urban parish of about a square mile comprising about 6,000 residents, with a regular Sunday congregation ranging between 65 and 100 adults with about 20 to 25 youngsters. Geographically the parish falls into two halves, with terraced housing to the north of the main arterial road and mixed, more substantial housing to the south. From its early days in the late nineteenth century the suburb had been very desirable, but with the demise of domestic service, the rise of suburban living and the high cost of running large properties, social change came during the post-war period. In consequence, many of these properties became bed-and-breakfast hotels, homes for the elderly and multiple occupancy dwellings, bringing into the neighbourhood a significant transient population. By the 1990s the familiar problems of inner urban areas such as social anonymity, drug abuse, theft, carelessness about the social fabric of the area and prostitution arrived. These changed the context within which the congregation was called to witness.

Hauerwas and living holiness

As we noted in Chapters 1–3, Hauerwas regards the Church as the context for Christian ethics. Sanctification is the way God transforms Christian communities so that they can faithfully witness to his reign and be formed to see and act as distinctively Christian communities.[2] He called this Church *A Community of Character*.[3] Characterized by distinctive and peaceable virtues, this Church embodies the ongoing story of the risen Jesus whose core plot is narrated in the Scriptures but whose story includes the contemporary, historic and eschatological Church. It is a Church whose presence is a prophetic sign of the present peaceable reign of Christ, a reign inclusive of the salvation of the cosmos. Its truthfulness is indicated by the character of its living and dying in ways which properly correlate with the way Christ lived and died. In Hauerwas's Church, people take precedence over texts, narratives or stories over ideas or ideology, and embodiment matters more than rhetoric.[4] The Church is a community of ordinary, often argumentative pilgrims being trained through the practices of worship and discipleship to see, describe, inhabit and engage with the world as Christians.[5] Such formation disposes them to embody the practices of Jesus which involve befriending the marginal, the stranger, the weak and the ordinary.[6] It also makes them into a distinctive historical and global community.[7] Furthermore, this formation generates real church growth since the Church only truly grows when God is the agent of growth. Hauerwas believes that much church growth thinking is often a form of anxious survivalism which seeks success in statistics.[8] Yet numerical congregational growth is not a necessary indication of a truthful Church.[9] Given his cruciform Christology he argues that faithful witness may sometimes lead to numerical decline and there may even be times when a catacomb existence is indicative of the truly catholic Church.[10]

Hauerwas's project does not provide a theory of Church. Rather, as a theologian or servant of the Church, he clarifies the significance of congregational practices, such as gathering for worship, confessing our sins together, praying together, listening to Scripture together, and caring for the sick. He helped me to see a way of living holiness in the performance of ordinary Christian practices. First, he flagged up the significance of public worship and how it forms our discipleship, deepens our loyalty to God and signifies our primary identity as Christians.[11] Second, he showed me how gathering together in worship trains Christians for mission.[12] Third, his exploration of narrative enabled me to see how the Church's witness formed part of the ongoing revelation of God's grace without diminishing the central and classical role of the canonical Scriptures. His approach showed how the divine story is still ongoing and how the little stories of particular Christian congregations contribute to this great epic of grace.[13] Fourth, his confidence in the present reign of Christ enabled me to trust in God as the one generating congregational growth and witness. Christians can confidently engage in mission, since wherever they go, Christ is already Lord. Fifth, his focus upon peaceableness suggested that the Christian community is called to befriend the stranger in whatever form that stranger appears. In God's community there is space for all who will respond. Consequently churches can risk being porous communities.

Living holiness: St Mary's sign

The challenge facing St Mary's in early 1993 was how to witness to the gospel in inner urban Doncaster. Our initial approach was to explore this vocation using three focal themes: worship, nurture and mission. In so doing we agreed from the outset that the congregation must be the agent of ministry and mission rather than simply the cleric and a few enthusiasts. We walked together as priest and people. In addition, the parish was not simply a responsibility: it was our mission field, the context of our particular adventure with God. We were to be a community sharing in God's mission in this particular context.

Consequently we consulted census records to see the profiles of those living in the parish and also mapped any active links we had with people in the area. We had many associate baptized 'members' whose connection with Church we wanted to foster and deepen. We also sought to find ways of becoming an open and porous community, hospitable to the baptized and seekers from wherever they came. The congregation aimed to become a community whose first gospel 'word' to the stranger was 'Welcome'; a 'Yes' rather than a 'No' or 'Not yet'. In order for this to happen we agreed that acts of worship must be accessible to the unchurched. Hence in Lent 1993 a 'Prayer and Gift' day took place to raise money for a new public address system and a large screen for the front of the church. Remarkably the money arrived, a member of the congregation built the screen and by the summer we were able to have book-free acts of worship, particularly at monthly all-age events during which baptisms took place. This did not mean that all acts of worship became screened. Instead, we developed a variety of services around a monthly pattern and challenged the congregation, with mixed success, to participate in all types of service. The challenge was to be trained in the art of loving the stranger.

To facilitate congregational formation we developed 'Root Groups' which met monthly on a Sunday afternoon for Evening Prayer, low-key Bible study and a tea party. Root Groups nourished fellowship, gave other church leaders an area of responsibility and also offered a mission and service structure for the church when leaflet drops, coffee rotas, hospitality and celebration events such as Harvest, Epiphany and Easter needed staffing. Furthermore, they provided a structure which configured the congregation towards growth, since they subdivided the pastoral and mission responsibilities of the congregation. They deepened fellowship so that mission together displayed a community which could welcome outsiders. We used music as a way of integrating the congregation so that singing together as a whole congregation fostered a sense of community cohesion. In addition, teaching sought not to pump people with abstract ideas about the Christian faith and practice but rather offered a creative and hermeneutical engagement with issues of the day. This was a conversation in which the Scriptures represented the core but not exhaustive wisdom of God since Christian tradition had a part to play. Nevertheless, learning had to be accessible, and so visual aids such as wallpaper sermons, drama and liturgical talks around the church were important to engage different learning styles.

As the local theologian my task was to help the congregation interpret our contemporary calling in the light of Scripture, tradition and sound learning. For example, the mid-week Communion service was often an occasion for education about complex theological issues. On one occasion, when discussing the fourth-century controversy between Arius and Athanasius, the congregation was split into two halves, one responsible for chanting '*Oti pote ouk en*' and the other '*Ouk pote oti ouk en*' (the Greek for 'There was a time when he did not exist' and 'There was not a time when he did not exist'). This dramatic pedagogy enabled the congregation to grasp why the Nicene Creed still matters, since if God is not in Christ then there is no salvation for the world. Similarly the controversy between Augustine of Hippo and Pelagius could be construed as Africa sorting out the English, with interesting implications for perspectives on their contemporary relationship.

We also sought to re-engage with the local community. Initiatives included developing visiting teams, having a generous approach to the occasional offices, improving links with local schools, starting mid-week and holiday clubs for youngsters, engaging with the local jazz club, patronizing local shops, and initiating a Christian Aid fair. In addition, we took part in noisy and colourful ecumenical street processions on Palm Sunday and during the summer. I tried to be a visible cleric by cycling and walking my dogs around the area. At the same time, Christians from overseas joined the congregation – many of whom worked at the Doncaster Royal Infirmary. This may partly have been due to the overseas experience of the vicarage family but was mainly due to the warm welcome they received from the congregation. This hospitality was reciprocated when we began to hold international evenings which enabled folk from overseas to share their exotic cuisine with local people. In addition, at one Remembrance Sunday we had testimonies about war and peace from an Afrikaner Anglican priest who had been a Black Sash activist in South Africa, and a Nigerian Anglican visitor. Consequently congregational growth happened as people of difference shared together vocally, in worship and by participating in various activities together.

Yet although we could attract large congregations to baptisms, major festivals and memorial services and were visiting assiduously, this did not translate into swift congregational growth. The congregation grew gradually until by 2000 the Electoral Roll was over 200 adults and we had over 60 youngsters linked to our mid-week clubs led by members of the congregation. However, visiting and other local initiatives were generating a greater sense of active responsibility for mission to the parish among a wide range of congregational members. This was deepened by a renovation project we embarked on in 1995, which aimed to improve the quality of the church premises as a contribution to this mission. The £100,000 needed for the renovation project was raised predominantly through regular 'Prayer and Gift' days, fundraising events, two major legacies and a grant from the diocese. The second of the two legacies came just as we reached the £75,000 mark and covered all the congregational giving to that point. Hence what individuals had prayerfully and sacrificially given was given back to the Christian community as a whole. This experience spoke a profound message about faith, Church and the character of being a giving community rooted in the grace of God.

Through such experiences the church was discovering the fruitfulness of an open, generous and yet challenging engagement with the gospel. Illustrative of this was the climax of my time at St Mary's when we took part in a community performance of the *Hopes and Dreams* musical as our major Millennium celebration.[14] This involved folk from a local dance school, the Jenny Riley School of Dance, three local primary schools, the South Yorkshire Crusade Choir, pupils from Danum Comprehensive School co-ordinated by Wheatley Churches Together. Over 1,200 people came to watch the performances and it was a remarkable sound to hear these folk, many of whom were not churchgoers, singing the Millennium Prayer. Here was an experience of popular piety given focus, space and embodiment. It reflected churches as singing societies welcoming the participation of other voices in the celebration of God's grace for all. Both the renovation project, its attendant giving and the returned money, together with *Hopes and Dreams*, gave the church a sense of life and drama, a testimony.

Reflections on congregational holiness

During the second half of my incumbency I began research on the work of Stanley Hauerwas as a way of trying to understand the vocation of the Church in contemporary society more clearly. Through reflecting on the story of St Mary's in conversation with his insights, a number of themes emerged relating to congregational holiness. First, Hauerwas's stress on the formative character of worship was being embodied in St Mary's story. Common and public worship was forming this congregation into an active and cohesive sign of God's grace, even though St Mary's congregation was quite diverse and by no means always a comfortable community. Common worship disposed people to listen to God together in order to discern the mission of God and thereby to join in with that mission. Second, Hauerwas's focus upon the character of the Church also found expression in this congregation. Their gathering for worship generated a quality of common life which was itself a witness to the love of God. During the 1990s the congregation grew numerically and in terms of its income. However, the key was the character of this growth and, in particular, the character of the community which was growing. Sanctification took precedence over statistics, especially given the ambiguous history of the Anglican Church in Doncaster. Third, Hauerwas's reflections on friendship and hospitality gave a theological rationale for congregational outreach, especially friendship of the marginal. Hospitality and regular visiting by members of the congregation, together with involvement in local concerns such as street prostitution and drug abuse, were indicative of the gospel. Fourth, this formation of life and greater confidence in mission changed the way the congregation looked at the context it was situated within. Instead, of being inward looking and defensive, they became more adventurous towards the neighbourhood. The congregation took risks in terms of outreach, giving, renovations, liturgies, delegation, shared ministry and the like. Following Jesus meant that the church was learning to live its life orientated and open to those on the fringe rather than following the Pharisaic defence of secure sacred space. Fifth, Hauerwas's attention to the significance of small gestures and signs of Christian commitment helped me to recognize the value of relatively small-scale patient initiatives such as support of Christian Aid projects, regular visiting, involvement with local schools and other local agencies. Such signs of commitment witness to God's faithfulness and love. Sixth, common worship, service and outreach fostered a greater sense of agency and shared ministry among the congregation. Seventh, the congregation faced the depth of Hauerwas's challenge to be a peaceable community when faced with local problems such as thieving, prostitution, drug abuse and social deprivation. Yet this commitment to peaceableness was evident when the church hall hosted a series of meetings chaired by the vicar between local people and the statutory bodies in order to make peace among a traumatized community as well as find a common way forward.

Conclusion

Hauerwas's work enabled me to see the way a particular congregation becomes a sign of the gospel within its distinctive context. It also flagged up the importance of belonging to the catholic Church of the past and present, since no congregation is an exhaustive sign of the gospel. Each needs other congregations, often quite different from each other, to bear witness to the universal gospel of grace. Nevertheless, the witness of a particular congregation, however fragile and fallible, represents a contingent and significant sign of the activity of God in the world. Four words summarize this congregational holiness: hearing, hallowing, hosting and hospitality.[15] St Mary's, Doncaster, was a church which, though attracting little public attention, sought to hear God's call in worship, to witness God's hospitable grace through mission, to hallow a local community through acts of Christian service, and thereby to host that community in the Eucharist of God's life. I believe it represented an embodied apologetic for the gospel in a way congruent with Hauerwas's understanding of the vocation of the Church.

Questions

- Can you see any connections between your own congregation's witness and the themes we have explored in Hauerwas's project?
- In what ways might congregational life obscure the sort of witness Hauerwas expects the Church to present?
- How does the story which your congregation lives speak of living holiness to those among whom it is situated?

Further reading

Hauerwas, Stanley and William H. Willimon, *Where Resident Aliens Live: Exercises for Christian Practices*, Nashville: Abingdon Press, 1996.

Thomson, John B., *Church on Edge? Practising Christian Ministry Today*, London: Darton, Longman & Todd, 2004.

Notes

1 This chapter is based on John B. Thomson, 'Conversational Church Growth', in Martyn Percy and Ian Markham (eds), *Why Liberal Churches Are Growing*, London: T. & T. Clark, 2006.

2 *Sanctify Them in the Truth: Holiness Exemplified*, Edinburgh: T. & T. Clark, 1998, pp. 215–16.

3 *A Community of Character: Toward a Constructive Christian Social Ethic*, 4th edn, Notre Dame: University of Notre Dame Press, 1986.

4 *A Community of Character*, p. 9, *In Good Company: The Church as Polis*, Notre Dame: University of Notre Dame Press, 1995, p. 58, *Sanctify Them*, p. 5. See also 'The Church as God's New Language', in *Christian Existence Today: Essays on Church, World and Living in Between*, Durham: The Labyrinth Press, 1988, pp. 47–65.

5 *Vision and Virtue: Essays in Christian Ethical Reflection*, Notre Dame: University of Notre Dame Press, 1981, p. 117.

6 *Christian Existence Today*, pp. 106–10 and 253–65.

7 See *A Community of Character*, pp. 105–6, *Against the Nations: War*

and Survival in a Liberal Society, Notre Dame: University of Notre Dame Press, 1992, pp. 112–13.

8 See 'What Would Pope Stanley Say', in *Christianity Today* (November/December 1998), pp. 2 and 7.

9 Stanley Hauerwas with Richard Bondi and David B. Burrell, *Truthfulness and Tragedy: Further Investigations into Christian Ethics*, 2nd edn, Notre Dame: University of Notre Dame Press, 1985, p. 6.

10 *Vision and Virtue*, p. 102.

11 See *In Good Company*, pp. 153–64.

12 Stanley Hauerwas, 'The Gesture of a Truthful Story', *Theology Today*, 42, July 1985, pp. 181–9, and *Wilderness Wanderings: Probing Twentieth-Century Theology and Philosophy*, Boulder: Westview Press, 1997, pp. 165–6.

13 *A Community of Character*, p. 40.

14 Paul Field and Stephen Deal, *Hopes and Dreams*, Eastbourne: Kingsway, 1999.

15 I am grateful to the Revd Graham Piggot for helping me to distil these four themes.

6

Sharing Holiness[1]

Themes from Hauerwas's work which inform this chapter are drawn from the following collections: *Unleashing the Scriptures*; *In Good Company: The Church as Polis*; and *Lord Teach Us: The Lord's Prayer and the Christian Life.*

Introduction

In the previous chapter I explored how a particular Christian community witnessed to the grace of God in a manner congruent with Hauerwas's thinking. It embodied a significant contextual sign of the gospel as it sought to live holiness. Faith was enfleshed, and this opened hearts to faith in a context where, for historical and cultural reasons, rhetoric is less trusted than tangible actions. As Hauerwas has reminded us, Christian witness depends upon accessible and tangible expressions of what living holiness means. The gospel message is first about bodies before it is about ideas. The voice of ordinary Christians, whose lives are visible to their neighbours, is the voice which carries conviction, and this is why the most effective mission and ministry happens when Christians live among those they witness to. In this chapter I want look at how Hauerwas's emphasis upon this way of sharing the Christian story is central to discipleship. His work has shown us that the way Christians walk with God affects their talk about God. Hence worship and discipleship training teach us how to speak our testimony.

Discipleship as sharing glory

Some years ago I was involved in developing *DOXA: A Discipleship Course*, which explores the formative character of worship.[2] The course emerged after Stanley Hauerwas set me thinking about discipleship development and liturgy. His work enriched my own understanding of Anglican discipleship and exposed its collaborative and political nature. In this chapter I want to look more closely at Hauerwas's understanding of discipleship, show its connection with worship, describe how this coheres with Anglican views of discipleship, and then indicate how *DOXA* facilitates such reflective discipleship development.

Hauerwas and discipleship

To be a disciple, as the first word of the Lord's Prayer reminds us, is to be part of a community, a travelling company living openly with God and one another. It is a social rather than a solitary journey.[3] As Hauerwas and Sage comment, 'Christianity [is] naming a journey of a people.'[4] Indeed, 'salvation, Christian salvation, is not some individual relationship between the individual and God. Rather, salvation is being drafted into an adventure, having had our lives commandeered by God to go on a journey called the Christian faith.'[5] To understand what this journey entails requires common reflection or reflection undertaken together. Only thus can the Church faithfully exhibit its commission 'to live our lives in such a way as to make visible to all the world that the holy God reigns … that God's newly won territory is us, those who pray "Hallowed be thy name"'.[6] As Hauerwas and Sage continue, 'we are a people whose moral lives are shaped liturgically. Our ethics is a by-product of our worship'[7] and our bodies display the legacy of this worship.[8] In short, living holiness is an outcome of faithful worship, since faithful worship enables God to transform Christians into holy people.

Discipleship is therefore formed through the practice of worship. In the essay, 'The Liturgical Shape of the Christian Life:

Teaching Christian Ethics as Worship',[9] Hauerwas notes that in liberal societies where the Church is on the back foot, 'nothing could be more salutary than being reminded that what makes Christians Christians is our worship of God'.[10] Indeed, 'what Christians think and do is hard to distinguish since both are constituted by God's praise'.[11] However, in order to become such a holy people, Christians need 'to be part of a community in which we discover the truth about our lives', for worship configures the Church to the source of truthfulness, God.[12]

Thus worship is a socially transforming experience in which we are recreated into people who can follow the light of God's grace in life and thereby recognize the world and its character.[13] Discipleship involves having our vision transformed as we worship so that we see the world as God's and inhabit this world appropriately. Such worship is public because private worship is prone to self-deception in a way that the communal liturgy can check. Equally a Christian understanding of God (theology) is a tradition-determined craft; it is a wisdom which we learn by being apprenticed to more experienced practitioners as we share in worship with them.[14] Engagement in a conversation with both the living Church and, through its corporate memory, with the legacy of the departed Church, enables contemporary disciples to locate themselves and their pilgrimage within the ongoing story of God.

Hauerwas teaches discipleship through liturgy. Indeed, 'the very fact that Christians must be gathered to worship suggests that the audience for Christian ethics must be those who have been shaped by the worship of God'.[15] For example, gathering together in Eucharistic worship displays the Church as a distinctive people with a distinctive ethic that anticipates the eschatological destiny of the cosmos.[16] While this sign is tarnished by denominationalism and violence, it still has contemporary force, since the Eucharist keeps pointing us to peaceableness as God's goal.[17] Likewise meditating together on the practices of Eucharistic worship means that 'for Christians it is never a question of whether to serve the world, but how they are to be of service in the world. We cannot forget that worship is the way God has given us to serve the world'.[18] It fosters discriminating skills in Christians to facilitate their faithful engagement with the state and with society.

Anglican discipleship

Hauerwas's attention to the liturgical shape of discipleship has affinities with Anglican conviction. Anglicans believe that how we pray shows what we believe and thus Anglican doctrine is embedded in liturgy. Summed up somewhat simplistically in the phrase '*Lex orandi, lex credendi*', this conviction regards beliefs not as a package of abstract ideas but as the communal practice of worship informed living. As Paul Avis comments, 'The (Anglican) Church's apprehension of truth is given, not through steadily more precise and accurate interpretations of its doctrinal formulae, but through its life of worship, prayer, fellowship, service and suffering.'[19] Furthermore, 'Anglicanism has adapted the principle that growth in holiness is a precondition for growth in the knowledge of God.'[20] This also chimes in well with Rowan Williams's interpretation of Richard Hooker's view of worship as 'more than the conveying of information to us; it is the renewal from within of what is possible for human experience'.[21] Similarly, Hooker's preference for corporate prayer over individual prayer and concern for the visibility of the Christian community as a communion open to the holiness of God's transforming power indicate a particular affinity between what Hauerwas proposes and Anglican practice.[22] According to Stephen Sykes, 'Hooker viewed worship as personal and dialogical … (and) Hooker's intention was to describe how effective the authorized liturgy was in forming and reforming Christians.'[23]

DOXA: a discipleship course

DOXA is founded on the centrality and formative character of Christian worship. The course invites Christians to distil the theological scripting and character of their discipleship from the practices of public Eucharistic worship. Consequently it requires no 'expert' to lead it, since the participants are already familiar with the practices reflected upon and hence there is no privileging of the more articulate or academic. There is also no control of the theological outcomes, since the practices themselves are theologically pregnant and thereby sufficiently generative of appropriate outcomes. However, in support of the core material, 30 or so folk from the Diocese of Sheffield have contributed short 'Share Spot Resources' on issues relevant to discipleship to supplement the practical wisdom of the participants. There are also short bibliographies for most sections. In contrast to many discipleship courses, *DOXA* does not intend to teach 'the faith' in the abstract. Instead, it hopes to enable a sharing of the faith of a particular Christian community in conversation with the catholic Church present and past.

DOXA: *talking the walk*

DOXA encourages ordinary Christians to become more aware of the effects of God's activity in their lives. It is about tracing holiness, the way God transforms the lives of disciples through worship. It privileges testimony since *DOXA* seeks to help people recognize how their own vision of life reflects God's work in them. In this way, it is hoped that Christians will grasp the significance of worship and become more confident in the grace of God active in their lives. By engaging with the *practices* of Eucharistic worship, the course seeks to avoid any sense that God can be imprisoned in a package of ideas or in the minds of any particular elite. Practices are the way communities exhibit, explore and develop their life. They are not about putting into practice ideas held in advance but more like a craftswoman developing the practical wisdom of weaving. Wisdom emerges in and through practising the craft.

Such practical Christian wisdom develops as Christians reflect upon how God is forming them as they practise their faith. The practices of common worship, such as gathering, confession, listening to Scripture, receiving the sacraments and the like, craft Christians into mature disciples since they train us how to live with God in life. In short, faith is formed and holiness is shared.

This is particularly important today when the institutional Church is under criticism both from without and from within. Criticism from without tends to focus upon supposedly authoritarian and manipulative tendencies within organized religion. Criticism from within tends to focus upon the need for a simpler, sharper and tidier faith, which can market itself in the public square to get a hearing. Both imply that human initiative and control are more fundamental than God's freedom to represent himself on his own terms. *DOXA* is an attempt to recognize the priority of God by locating discipleship development in the experience of attention, listening and gazing; that is, in the context of active, open response. There is no attempt to determine in advance what God's freedom will disclose, save that the way Christians have listened to God in the past guides and disposes us to recognize the voice of God in our own context. Thus the 'Share Spot Resources' are opportunities to listen to how fellow travellers are reflecting on Christian discipleship. They are not the final word on the theme, nor are they exhaustive accounts.

The course flags up the apologetic significance of ordinary Christians. It pays attention to what emerges as God works in the midst of ordinary living. Historically, it was in the monasteries and then in the parishes that this living and practical holiness had its home. In the medieval universities a more reason-focused theology developed, and with the advent of printing and increasing specialization this has taken much of the territory of theology. However, rich theological wisdom is lost if we are not able to hear the dialects of Christians beyond the academy or seminary. *DOXA* therefore explicitly seeks to encourage ordinary Christians to share their own theological testimonies. Such sharing fosters conversations as participants discover the differences in their respective theological testimonies and engage with the Share Spots.

DOXA is not about teaching the liturgy so much as disclosing how the liturgy opens up Christians to God. As such, those who have been Christians for some time will find that it enables them to distil the meaning of their discipleship and become more consciously aware of what God has been doing in their lives. In addition, those new to the faith can begin to grasp the shape of Christian living as they allow the liturgy to do its work. This approach is open-ended since the wisdom that emerges as ordinary Christians reflect upon their worship practices is ongoing, diverse and disciplined by those practices rather than by a controlling elite, clerical or scholarly. Scholarly and clerical wisdom therefore serves the Church by assisting ordinary Christians to locate their own discipleship dialects within the wider Christian language. It does not determine that language.

Such an approach acts as a catalyst, making possible a form of conversational theology which can continually sound the depths of congregations or participants. Like all conversations, detailed outcomes are not guaranteed in advance. There is an element of surprise involved, for God's activity and freedom are assumed by the course. I believe it represents an attractive way of learning of God at a time when many inside and beyond the institutional Church are hostile to forms of control and closure by the powerful. In contrast to approaches which seek to tell people what to believe or which give the impression of possessing all the answers to faith questions in advance, *DOXA* presumes that faith is a relational and timeful journey rather than a fixed ideology. Hence the wisdom and holiness of God are constantly being discovered and developed, and fresh insights are emerging relative to God's work in us.

DOXA therefore has an evangelistic dimension. Worship is evangelism in the sense that God-with-us is always gospel, good news. Exploring what God is doing among us as we worship illuminates further the character and transforming power of the gospel. God refuses to be absent from among those gathering in his name. Likewise this approach restores the link between belonging and believing.[24] Belonging is seen to be vital to the ongoing discipleship development since worship shapes our discipleship. We are, after all, participating consciously in God, and, in the language of the Eastern Church, being divinized. As this happens, others see the difference Christ makes in the world and in our lives.

Conclusion: sharing holiness

DOXA enables Christians to recover confidence in their testimony and the way this testimony, in conversation with others present and past, can deepen discipleship and generate a form of pew theology. It is about tracing what God is doing in particular communities of faith as they are formed through the practices of common worship. Such liturgical formation, as Hauerwas's work and Anglican practice demonstrate, enables Christians to become theologically reflective disciples whose formation and understanding are inextricably wedded together. Furthermore, it undermines any private notion of discipleship and any divorce between discipleship and active participation in a worshipping community.

Questions

- How does your church's pattern of worship enable you to speak about the Christian faith?
- In what ways is your discipleship enriched by communal worship?
- What does practising your faith mean to you?
- How might theologians serve the Church better?
- How could you become a more reflective Christian practitioner?

Notes

1 This chapter includes material from the introduction to *DOXA: A Discipleship Course*, London: Darton, Longman & Todd, 2007.

2 See *DOXA*.

3 For an exploration of this diverse company and its character see *In Good Company: The Church as Polis*, Notre Dame: University of Notre Dame Press, 1995, and William H. Willimon and Stanley Hauerwas, with Scott C. Sage, *Lord Teach Us: The Lord's Prayer and the Christian Life*, Nashville: Abingdon Press, 1996, p. 28.

4 *Lord Teach Us*, p. 13.

5 *Lord Teach Us*, p. 21.

6 *Lord Teach Us*, p. 44.

7 *Lord Teach Us*, p. 47.

8 *Lord Teach Us*, p. 50.

9 Stanley Hauerwas, 'The Liturgical Shape of the Christian Life: Teaching Christian Ethics as Worship', *In Good Company*, pp. 153–64. A fuller exploration of this approach can be found in Stanley Hauerwas and Samuel Wells (eds), *The Blackwell Companion to Christian Ethics*, Oxford: Blackwell, 2006.

10 *In Good Company*, p. 153.

11 *In Good Company*, p. 154.

12 *In Good Company*, p. 155.

13 *In Good Company*, p. 156.

14 *In Good Company*, p.158.

15 *In Good Company*, p.157.

16 *In Good Company*, p. 162.

17 *In Good Company*, p. 163.

18 *In Good Company*, p. 163.

19 Paul Avis, *Ecumenical Theology and the Elusiveness of Doctrine*, London: SPCK, 1986, p. 43.

20 Paul Avis, *Ecumenical Theology*, p. 94.

21 Rowan Williams, 'Hooker the Theologian', *Journal of Anglican Studies*, 1, 2003, p. 109.

22 For this commitment to visibility see Paul Avis, *The Anglican Understanding of the Church: An Introduction*, London: SPCK, 2000, pp. 76–7. On Hooker's commitment to the primacy of corporate worship see Stephen W. Sykes (ed.), *Authority in the Anglican Communion: Essays Presented to Bishop John Howe*, London, Ontario: Anglican Book Centre, 1987, pp. 101–2.

23 Sykes, *Authority*, pp. 101–2.

24 Grace Davie, *Religion in Britain Since 1945: Believing without Belonging*, Oxford: Oxford University Press, 1994.

7

Discerning Holiness[1]

Themes from Hauerwas's work which inform this chapter are drawn from the following collections: *A Community of Character Toward a Constructive Christian Social Ethic*; and *Unleashing the Scripture: Freeing the Bible from Captivity to America.*

Introduction

My discipleship was formed in the evangelical wing of Anglicanism, a tradition deeply committed to Scripture as the focal matrix of Christian practice. Yet evangelical Anglicans are evangelicals within Anglicanism, a tradition rooted in the work of Cranmer and Hooker, which situated the public reading and interpretation of Scripture within a liturgical and hence ecclesial context. Anglican evangelicals therefore explore Scripture in the Church, the community which lives explicitly in the story the Scriptures speak of. In discipleship the scriptural and corporate belong together.[2] In addition, evangelical commitment to personal holiness expects Christian discipleship to witness to the holiness of God revealed in Jesus Christ. Scripture and living holiness are central to Anglican evangelical witness.

Consequently, congruent with Hauerwas, Anglican evangelicalism properly recognizes that living holiness, communal discipleship and scriptural discernment belong together.[3] The stories of Scripture as stories are not to be used as pretexts for an abstract or private account of faith. We inhabit these stories as the Church rather than mining them for private and abstract gospel gems. In addition, their historical and narrative character implies the ongoing presence of a community whose life and story both connects with and displays the force of these stories in contemporary life. The Scriptures are not a closed account of the work of God in the world. Furthermore, individualistic interpretations of the stories are inadequate, since our situatedness and consequently limited perspective mean that we cannot hope to achieve an accurate understanding of those stories. Individualism underestimates the possibility of misunderstanding. A more catholic and doxological approach to interpretation reduces this problem.

In this chapter I shall argue that the practice of reading and interpreting Scripture in common worship conditions Christians to hear the voice of God in contemporary life. To do this, I will begin by demonstrating why Hauerwas is correct to assert that the Church rather than the individual is the interpreter of Scripture. Then I will suggest how the Scriptures themselves imply that communal living holiness is intrinsic to the Scriptures' revelatory role and will illustrate this using the early chapters of Genesis as a case study. In so doing, my intention is to show how Christians interpret Scripture within the Church and are formed to interpret it corporately. In particular I want to underscore Hauerwas's contention that Christianity is fundamentally about a people inhabiting the story of God rather than an ideology or set of beliefs about God held independently of the Church. Scripture is always Scripture in the Church and has to be interpreted communally and in the light both of the Church's past and its destiny. Consequently a truthful interpretation of Scripture requires a holy community of interpreters since it is God's grace active in the Church which sifts and forms it to grasp the way the story of God is to be understood. Holiness and hermeneutics belong together.

Making the Church visible in our reading of Scripture

Hauerwas has reminded us that it is the existence of the Church which underscores the authority of Scripture, since without this community Scripture would be simply another series of ancient texts for academics.[4] Thus the reading of the Bible as Scripture, rather than simply as ancient biblical texts, is properly undertaken in and as the Church. Indeed, Hauerwas is concerned that Christians have 'allowed Scripture to be separated from Church-centred practice'.[5] This has generated abstract readings of Scripture which uncritically re-contextualize it within the social order of those reading it. In consequence, Scripture loses its interpretative community and, in North Atlantic societies, becomes prey to anarchic individualism with no regard for any communal accountability and training.[6] Furthermore, reading Scripture as Scripture requires the Church to give the Scripture meaning since the Church not only forms disciples to read Scripture truthfully, but also represents the embodiment of that community which explicitly inhabits the story of Scripture.[7] Indeed, as Hauerwas comments, 'a sermon is Scriptural when it inscribes a community into an ongoing Christian narrative'.[8]

Thus reading Scripture is disciplined and given its primary context by liturgy rather than by the academy or solitary student. Performance of the liturgy trains Christians to interpret the story as those who worship the God the Scriptures speak of. In such contexts Scripture is revelatory since, as the community gathers to worship and listen to Scripture, their particular vocation in the mission of God is clarified. Furthermore, an explicitly ecclesial reading of Scripture is not only essential but is called for by the character and narrative structure of the Scriptures themselves. As Edith Humphrey argues in *Fanning the Flame* – using Tom Wright's dramatic architecture of Scripture configured around the great themes of Creation, Fall, Israel, Messiah, Church and Parousia – Scripture offers us a grand narrative within which to locate our own stories.[9] In addition, 'our reading and understanding … has been shaped by the ongoing Christian tradition, and deliberately so, since the Scriptures themselves intimate that this is fitting'.[10] Reading Scripture is always a conversation within the Church.

Stanley Hauerwas has also shown us that the Scriptures self-confessedly invite a faithful community to participate in the divine story as agents rather than merely passengers. The biblical story is the story of God's relationship with creation. It is the most encompassing and fundamental of stories engulfing all other narratives within itself. Hence it embraces and goes beyond the Scriptures in the sense that it is inclusive of all that God is about, some of which is yet to happen. What the Scriptures do is delineate the character and shape of the story by narrating the identity and mission of its principal agent, God, in his relationship with creation. The biblical story is finished in the sense that its character and shape are correlative to this God and God's definitive self-revelation in Jesus Christ. However, it is not exhaustive since it allows space for further enrichment and corruption, since the invitation to be agents in the story offers a degree of relative freedom and contribution to creation, both human and non-human. Hauerwas encourages us to explore the way we are enfolded into the biblical story rather than trying to fit the biblical story into some prior explanation of human existence. In consciously participating in the biblical story, the faithful community contributes significantly to the sub-plots of that story, whose focal plot is the redemption of the cosmos by Jesus Christ, God-with-us enfleshed and now glorified.

Scripture, Christ and Christ's body

The Scriptures are self-confessedly incomplete or underdetermined, not in terms of their focal salvific Christological plot, but in terms of how that plot engages and is embodied by the community which it brings to birth.[11] By 'incomplete' or 'underdetermined' therefore, we mean that the story they speak of awaits the *parousia* for its consummation.[12] This offers space for present and future contributions. As Sue Patterson argues, 'underdeterminedness [is] at the heart of an incarnational Christology' and suggests that a pluralist Church reflecting a rainbow of stories points to the universality of the gospel.[13] This does not threaten the sufficiency of Christ as the full and final revelation of God. It implies that what Christ *means* extends beyond the historical Jesus to embrace the cosmic Christ with whom the Church is intrinsically connected as body to head.[14] What Christ exhaustively means will only be completely known at the *parousia*. Hence the story of Christ is ongoing even though Christ is the finished, that is, definitive Word of God.[15] This is the living holiness of the Church.

This consequence of the resurrection and ascension of Christ implies that what Christ is becoming, though configured around the historical identity of Jesus, is open to enrichment, as the body of Christ is led by the Spirit into all truth.[16] As Gerard Loughlin argues, 'the church is the community that tells Christ's story by being itself the continuing story of Christ; embodying the story of Christ in the circumstances of its day'.[17] The embrace of the Gentiles and the changed understanding of the Torah in Paul are indicative of this. The Scriptures, while representing the Christologically definitive way that salvation pathway is to be walked, do not delineate in advance all that will emerge on that journey, as we argued in Chapter 4. Christ, as the rule for the Church's reading of Scripture, is only realized in the practice of faithful reading.[18] However, the timeful and narrative character of these Scriptures suggests that walking in this way will dispose the Church to see new truths immanent in all that the Christ represents and is becoming. Some of these new truths may appear to conflict with earlier understandings, as in the case of female leadership in Church and society or the possibility of limited forms of usury within nominally Christian societies. However, the fact that analogous changes were present from the earliest days of Christianity means that ethical change is consistent with the possibilities implied by both the narrative dynamics of these Scriptures and by scriptural precedent.

Thus the Pentecost gift of the Spirit to the Church is the ground for the Church's capacity to discern where Christ's truth is active in contemporary contexts, as we argued in Chapters 1 and 3. Such discernment will also be contextual, since the way Christ is known to different communities will have its own particularity reflective of the incarnation itself. The relationship between holy discipleship and the ancestors or circumcision rites of South African Xhosa culture will require a particular Christological discernment whose outcome may be quite alien to north European Christians. Equally, the relationship between holy discipleship and sexual identity may be discerned in north European contexts in a way quite different from that in traditional Xhosa culture. What enables such diverse discernments to remain in conversation is that both seek to be accountable to what the Church has learned of Christ so far on its Spirit-infused journey. This Christ is definitively but not exhaustively narrated in the Scriptures and is attended to in common worship.

Hauerwas shows us that through worship the Christian community develops the skills to listen to God. This is a communal activity, and through these practices Christians are formed into a faithful, holy people who can read the Scriptures truthfully. Such common worship does not necessarily imply interpretative unanimity. Rather, it requires mutual yet accountable trust that the Church, in different contexts, has different challenges to face and therefore distinctive discerning to do. Argument and disagreement will be inevitable given the finite and fallible character of the Church. Nevertheless, this Christian '*phronesis*' or practical wisdom is more reflective of the implications of the incarnation than the temptations of abstract and timeless theorizing about the ways of God with life. It is about openness and listening rather than a closed system of ideas.[19]

All this suggests that – prior to the *parousia* – discernment of provisional prophetic narrations of Christ's contemporary identity is possible. For example, in the struggle against apartheid in South Africa, the majority of Christians argued that Christ was on the side of the anti-apartheid struggle rather on the side of biblically justified racism. Similarly Wilberforce and Shaftsbury saw Christ as involved in the liberation of slaves and, more ambiguously, many Christians have come to accept that a degree of usury is compatible with Christian discipleship. All these discernments represent challenges to past interpretations of certain biblical texts or traditions. To their protagonists their legitimacy resides in their consistency with the historical story of Jesus mediated to us through the New Testament. This Jesus is not locked into the past, or into ancient texts, but as risen and ascended is present to creation by the Spirit in such a way that the story of God is ongoing and developing. The Church is charged with both discerning how the risen, ascended Christ is active by the Spirit in creation affairs and with allowing its life to embody the contemporary Christ.

The Christian community, both as discerner and participant in the ongoing story, is vital to the way the story is being told and will finally be told at the End we call the *parousia*. This is because the Christian community, as the *body of Christ*, represents and contributes to an embodied apologetic for the story of God. As Hauerwas argues, 'sharing in an interpretative community produces a common life making Scripture intelligible. Scripture is not intelligible on its own.'[20] In short, the Church, as an interpreting community discerning Christ's contemporary action in its life and in the world, witnesses and, in some way, substantiates the meaning of the story of Scripture since the ecclesial and scriptural stories co-inhere.

God and God's story – narrative, community and creation

The dynamic character of this participation in the divine story is reflected in the naming of the early Christian community as the community of the Way. As well as implying a destiny, such a description implies that pilgrimage, journey and movement are characteristic of discipleship rather than the distillation and articulation of a timeless Christian ideology or theology. As such it also suggests that the past does not contain the totality of the future, however indicative it may be. Such a dynamic view of Christian discipleship, furthermore, is consonant with the dynamic character of creation and history. Scientific and historical research increasingly describe their findings within dynamic categories rather than using the static ones of the ancient world. It is as if the narrative character of the Scriptures finds echoes in the narrative character of creation and history.[21]

Furthermore, the space opened up in creation for a serious and genuine participation in the divine story by that creation (particularly humankind), together with the dynamic identity of God implied by the Trinity, suggests that God is not outside the story as some timeless stability. Rather, God, through the Spirit, participates in creation and thereby is involved in the social and thus linguistic world, without being reduced to an object in or of this world.[22] Nevertheless, God's story, which engulfs all other stories, is not a totalitarian narrative but one which emerges in and through this relationship. Indeed, precisely because of God's own character, the story is underdetermined; that is, it has real space for active and morally accountable participation by God's creatures. Living holiness involves being invited into God's story. God's sovereignty is not expressed in the crushing of creation, but in the offering to creation of genuine moral space for response and contribution. God's power is correlative to God's character. The Scriptures, by representing the ways of God with creation in narrative terms, invite this way of walking and conversing with Christ. It is this journey, as Hauerwas suggests, which enables the Church to contribute to the story of Christ as his body 'the organized form of Jesus' story'.[23]

Such a narrative understanding of the relationship of God with creation is further delineated as we reflect upon the implications of the incarnation of the *Logos* as Jesus of Nazareth. Here we note the character of God's self-expression within the limitations and horizons of time and space. That Jesus engaged with the Torah, Wisdom traditions and Prophets as a Jew within the horizon and norms of that era should indicate for us that it is precisely from within the horizons of our own contexts that we do the same with the scriptural traditions. This is the 'scandal of particularity'. In order for all to be redeemed, God acted in the detail so that no detail or depth could escape his grasp. It also warns us against seeking a timeless blueprint for social order in the Bible, since the incarnation is a particular narrative exposition of God, not an abstract timeless exposition of God. Christ is Saviour not because he and his work transcend time in idealist terms, but because they inhabit and redeem time from within, thereby respecting the created order and its timeful character. In consequence, all of time is not obliterated but seen as the environment within which this salvation can be known.

Thus, to expect that we can read the Scriptures exactly as Jesus did is to presume, falsely, that both he and we can escape from the character of existence in time. We can certainly seek to follow the direction of Jesus' interpretation of Scripture, which he promised would continue and develop under the guidance of the Spirit given to but not contained in the Church.[24] However, since Jesus wrote no book, the mediated character of his story itself indicates that the interpretation of Scripture for today will be through the presence of the risen, ascended Christ in his Church by his Spirit, rather than simply by assuming that we can jump across time and space to engage immediately with the Jesus of history. The image of the empty tomb is vital here, since it speaks of a Christ who is not contained in any temporal space any longer, whether this be geographic or textual. Likewise, the form and character of the Scriptures suggest that in Christ by the Spirit the Christian community is embraced as an active participant within the life of the Trinity. The narrative of the ascension involves the welcoming by the Father of all that Christ's story represents and will represent.

Discerning the word of God involves listening for the voice of the Spirit-mediated ubiquitous Christ, whose body Paul calls the Church, that community which historically and today participates in his risen life. As Hauerwas has shown, worship, therefore, becomes the environment wherein the Word communicates God's prophetic word to us. The word of the Lord for a given community at a particular time is discerned by that community as it gathers to attend to the Word of God present by the Spirit in worship, Scripture and Sacrament. However, any particular ecclesial gathering is also webbed into the wider Christian community. It must attend to the way that community also is listening and responding, and part of the role of liturgy is to enable this listening to be common rather than at the mercy of particular interest groups within a congregation or diocese. It is sobering to recall that Afrikaner Christians in the Dutch Reformed Church believed that a unilateral reading of Scripture could locate racial differences in the created order and thereby theologically underwrite apartheid, despite the dissent of the wider Christian community, including their own Reformed tradition.

Church, wisdom and Scripture: interpreting Genesis 1

Listening for the word of God today involves a careful attention to how, according to the Scriptures, our ancestors listened for God's word in their time and context. For example, the creation account of Genesis 1 offers an illustration of the community of Judah exiled in Babylon hearing the best 'scientific' wisdom of their captors and locating this within the story of their God. Furthermore, by placing this account of creation at the beginning of their 'history', the ancient redactors integrated what later would be called the books of nature and of revelation. In consequence, God's contemporary word meets the Church in a critical reflection upon the best available human wisdom concerning the cosmos refracted through the experience of the community's worship of God through history. In short, this involves the Church discerning what of contemporary human wisdom is consonant with the worship of God in Christ today and what is not. This 'way' of interpreting life and God does not seek to escape the conclusions of human wisdom. Rather, it repositions and interrogates them from the perspective of the people of God. It thereby avoids the deception of ideology, which suggests that ideas can be held in a timeless and context-less way. By masking the fact that we are in time and located in a multi-contextual environment, ideological readings deceptively ignore the more challenging interpretive task. They can even imply that how we read these chapters is identical to the way they would have been construed by their initial authors.[25] Not only does this subvert the implications of the incarnation and history but it hides the place of the Church in the reading of Scripture.

Such a way of discerning the call of God has enabled most Christians to take on board the insights of contemporary science. It is clearly anachronistic to suggest that the reflections and stories of Genesis 1—11 give temporally advanced examples of modern science or history. However, looking at the way the authors of Genesis 1 attended to God helps us analogously to engage with new insights from wherever they emerge. This approach can also be used to help us engage with other Scriptures. The stories of Genesis 2—10, the Torah, the Prophets, the Wisdom traditions, the Psalms, Jesus himself and the New Testament are all representative of a community at different stages on its way before God. In addition, the composition of some of these Scriptures indicates that Israel was open to receiving wisdom from beyond the contours of the community of faith.[26] The Scriptures are not resources to be mined for abstract beliefs, nor are they static fixtures to lock the Church into the past. They dispose us to listen for God today in ways analogous to – and alert to – what has gone before. They are our tradition and, as Gadamer has reminded us, tradition is the prejudice that enables us to understand.[27] This renders the Christian community a community open to the new and invites the Church, as an interpreting community, to discern when that new is present. This is a decision which, in Anglican conviction, involves common worship – the attentive wisdom-seeking of the whole community, rather than simply the clergy or the theological elite.[28]

Narrative hermeneutics is liberating but also disturbing, since it may involve recognizing that contemporary listening to God can be in apparent conflict with earlier interpretations. Nevertheless, it is not about abstract rights and wrongs, but about contextual response whose ultimate meaning is not given until the *parousia*. As shown in the cases of slavery, the place of women in Church and society, usury, male circumcision and food laws, the Church at different times in its history is able to discern that what was a word for an earlier generation is a word for today in a different way. It may be that this approach will offer a way forward in the debate over same-sex relationships.[29] This is because descriptions of reality including moral evaluation do not remain static, since those doing the describing and the context of the describing are both in time. There is a constant re-describing of what is going on, a re-narrating of the story so far. Tradition may help to stabilize the fluidity of the interpretation by reminding the hermeneutical community that it is what it is because of its past. Tradition, however, does not excuse that community from its contemporary task to listen for God in the present. Indeed, as indicated in our discussion of Genesis 1, this tradition disposes Christians to listen to the best wisdom of the day and carefully to locate this wisdom within its ongoing interpretation of the story of God indicated by that tradition. For example, the way sex and sexuality have been scientifically re-narrated in western societies over the past two centuries requires careful discernment by the Church rather than by sectional groups or individuals to ensure that if there is a word of the Lord here, it is faithfully heard.

Conclusion

Hauerwas has reminded us that we can only properly interpret Scripture as the Church. Indeed, the way we walk with God informs how we hear God's word. Sanctification therefore affects how we understand Scripture, since it forms us into holy interpreters more attuned to the speech of God and thereby able to discern where the pathway for living holiness lies, the next stage in the story of God. Consequently, instead of expecting to discern a singular interpretation of the 'word of the Lord' independent of time and place, contextual meditation on the Scriptures will generate a more plural set of responses. This approach, I believe, is consistent with the shape and character of Scripture itself as an open narrative of God's ways with the world, whose consummation is still outstanding but whose core plot pivots around the saving work of Jesus Christ, the incarnate God-with-us. It is therefore Scripture in the Church, which will enable us to hear God's word to us today, rather than Scripture independent of the Church.

Questions

- How persuasive is Hauerwas's view that we can only read and interpret the Scriptures as the Church?
- How could your church better learn to read Scripture together?
- How might your worship and life together as a Christian community influence your interpretation of Scripture?

- What do you understand by the phrase 'Scripture is an open narrative'?
- What does it mean for you to inhabit the story of Scripture?

Notes

1 My thanks to the Revd Dr Andrew Goddard and to the Revd Canon Professor Martyn Percy for reading this chapter and offering constructive comments. A version of this chapter originally appeared as 'Time for Church? Evangelicals, Scripture and Conversational Hermeneutics', in *Anvil*, 21.4, 2005, pp. 245–57.

2 Angela Tilby, in Steven Croft (ed.), *Mission-Shaped Questions*, London: Church House Publishing, 2008, p. 80.

3 See *Unleashing the Scripture: Freeing the Bible from Captivity to America*, Nashville: Abingdon Press, 1993.

4 *A Community of Character: Toward a Constructive Christian Social Ethic*, 4th edn, Notre Dame: University of Notre Dame Press, 1986, pp. 53–71, 53.

5 *Unleashing the Scripture*, p. 9.

6 *Unleashing the Scripture*, pp. 32–6.

7 *Unleashing the Scripture*, p. 36.

8 *Unleashing the Scripture*, p. 42.

9 Edith Humphrey, 'Kairos and Chronos: Meditations on Revelation, God's Word and God's World', in Paul Gardner, Chris Wright and Chris Green (eds), *Fanning the Flame: Bible, Cross and Mission: Meeting the Challenge in a Changing World*, Grand Rapids: Zondervan, 2003, pp. 105–8.

10 Humphrey, 'Kairos and Chronos', p. 110.

11 Christology is the study of Christ.

12 The *parousia* is popularly known as the Second Advent or Second Coming of Christ.

13 Sue Patterson, *Realist Christian Theology in a Postmodern Age*, Cambridge: Cambridge University Press, 1999, p. 151.

14 See Colossians 1.15–20.

15 See Rowan Williams, *On Christian Theology*, Oxford: Blackwell, 2000, p. 173.

16 John 16.12.

17 Gerard Loughlin, *Telling God's Story: Bible Church and Narrative Theology*, Cambridge: Cambridge University Press, 1996, pp. 82–4.

18 *Telling God's Story*, p. 119.

19 Hans-Georg Gadamer, *Truth and Method*, 2nd edn, London: Sheed & Ward, 1993, pp. 20–2.

20 Stanley Hauerwas, 'Interpreting the Bible as a Political Act', *Religion and Intellectual Life*, 6, 1989, p. 137.

21 Daniel W. Hardy, *God's Ways with the World: Thinking and Practising Christian Faith*, Edinburgh: T. & T. Clark, 1996, pp. 91–130.

22 Brad J. Kallenberg, 'Unstuck from Yale: Theological Method After Lindbeck', *Scottish Journal of Theology*, 50, 1997, pp. 201, 209–13.

23 *A Community of Character*, p. 41.

24 John 16.12–15.

25 For the disappearance of the author in the transmission of texts see Paul Ricœur, *Hermeneutics and the Human Sciences*, 2nd edn, ed. and trans. by John B. Thompson, Cambridge: Cambridge University Press, 1982, pp. 91–4.

26 James Barr, *Biblical Faith and Natural Theology*, Oxford: Clarendon Press, 1993, pp. 150 and 205.

27 Gadamer, *Truth and Method*, pp. 267–77.

28 On the liberation of the laity and the role of Scripture in the reformed Church of England as envisaged by Richard Hooker, the sixteenth-century English Reformer, see Paul Avis, *Anglicanism and the Christian Church: Theological Resources in Historical Perspective*, Edinburgh: T. & T. Clark, 1989, pp. 60–7.

29 This is why the approach offered in Timothy Bradshaw (ed.), *The Way Forward? Christian Voices on Homosexuality and the Church*, London: Hodder & Stoughton, 1997, must continue for ecclesial rather than merely pragmatic reasons.

8

Cultivating Holiness[1]

The principal themes from Hauerwas which inform this reflection are drawn from the following collections. *Truthfulness and Tragedy: Further Investigations into Christian Ethics*; *A Community of Character Toward a Constructive Christian Social Ethic*; *Christian Existence Today: Essays on Church*; *World and Living in Between*; *In Good Company: The Church as Polis*; and *Sanctify Them in the Truth: Holiness Exemplified.*

Hauerwas and a growing Church

Stanley Hauerwas's approach to Christian ethics is rooted in notions of character, community, narrative and performance. Consequently his approach to the way the Christian community both lives and grows is fundamentally organic. The Church is a living community located in different cultures and contexts which embodies the great story of God's love and call. Growth is consequently about divine cultivation rather than human manipulation, and cultivation is a metaphor which roots growth within an organic and indeed narrative framework. In consequence, Christian ethics is the way the Christian community lives its life open to God, which entails understanding the story and ethos of this community and how this story illuminates this community's future. Hauerwas flags up this approach in his earliest work, such as the 1977 essay 'From System to Story: An Alternative Pattern for Rationality in Ethics'.[2] Here Hauerwas and his co-writer David Burrell argue that contemporary ethics, the way a community lives its life, ignored the significance of narrative in favour of securing a rational and abstract foundation for ethics. What this neglected was an awareness that

> the kind of decisions we confront, indeed, the very way we describe a situation, is the function of the kind of character we have. And character is not acquired through decisions, though it may be confirmed and qualified there; rather it is acquired through the beliefs and dispositions we have come to possess … it is our contention … that it is character, in as much as it is displayed by a narrative, that provides the context necessary to pose the terms of a decision, or to determine whether a decision should be made at all.[3]

For Christians, this narrative is the story of God reconciling the universe to himself through Christ, a story now embodied in the ongoing life of the Christian community and which is fundamentally about the particulars of that community.

Consequently the 'I' or 'We' making decisions and acting in the world, is not an atomistic 'I' or 'We', as envisaged by the influential eighteenth-century philosopher Kant, but rather is a narrative 'I' or 'We'. Hence we discover our identity through participating in a series of interconnecting stories as part of a community which shares a common language. Thus 'all our notions are narrative dependent, including the notion of rationality'.[4] In contrast, the philosopher Kant's ethics flattened everything out by seeking to conform all to abstract and systematic norms which deceptively purported to represent objective truths.[5] It represented the eighteenth-century Enlightenment's quest for certainty in a contingent world and it achieved this by denying that very contingency which it sought to transcend. Facts and values thereby became divorced and distinctive identity was lost in the stampede towards timeless uniformity. In doing this, it subverted critical insights for Christian living or ethics.

Hauerwas and Burrell also argue that this now standard approach to ethics regarded human beings as examples of a type which could be generalized about in abstract terms. Furthermore, it allowed these generalizations to be used for predictive purposes. From such sociology a systematic picture could be built up which paid scant attention to the particularities and contexts of the people involved. Their character, that contingent distillation of their particular narrative identity, was ignored and instead they were simply resources for a system whose application could be expressed in any context at any time. In preference for the details of their storied identity, a 'thick' description of their narrative, this approach privileged a superficial and under-explored identity masking narrative depth in favour of a superficial description of their identity.[6] As a result it lost sight of the significance of the word 'Christian' in the phrase 'Christian ethics'.

In contrast, they argue that encouraging the Church to fulfil its destiny in God's mission is fundamentally about worship and transformation, about cultivating holy communities. The Church is a community participating in the ongoing story of God's transformation of creation, an insight underscored by the narrative shape of Scripture and in the history of the Church. It is in and through this ongoing story of Scripture and Church that the mission of God is discerned and described in the world.[7] Similarly, it is in and through this ongoing story that contemporary mission, ministry, church growth and development are faithfully cultivated. Indeed, these are integrated within and integral to the way the story is both manifested and told. As Peter Collins comments, such 'narratives are … embodied and [are] negotiated in dialogue with local history and congregational structures'.[8] The story manifests itself in ways appropriate to the various contexts that churches are called to inhabit. Thus there is a plurality about the narratives which faithfully expresses 'the story of God's being as gift, as self gift establishing and enlivening the world'.[9] Consequently, fostering the conditions for mission is primarily about understanding and interpretation rather than explanation and technique.[10] It involves the art of cultivation rather than the technique of method, the organic rather than the systematic.

Growth at ground level

One of the advantages of having lived in different parts of the world is realizing that what grows well in one context does not thrive in another. As a child I was fascinated that apples grew in England whereas bananas didn't, and that in Uganda the reverse was true. Whereas cars and TVs functioned in similar ways whether in England or Uganda, living organisms flourished relative to local conditions. Organisms could not simply be transplanted in the way that technology made possible for inanimate objects. Part of my present role involves fostering ministerial and congregational development across the Diocese of Sheffield in England. To this end I have visited clergy to talk with them about ministry and mission. In conversation with more than 100 I have discovered considerable differences in understanding and expectations, as one would expect within an Anglican diocese. Most are agreed that traditional models of ministry and mission seem to deliver less, though many remain committed to them. On the other hand, alternative models of ministry and mission using analogies from industry, business or the public services are met with ambivalence since they seem to lose something vital about the character of Church as a divinely constituted community and of ministry as a practice rather than a technique or theory.

I suspect that part of the struggle with the latter is because such analogies seem to reduce the Church to one institution or organization comparable with others. As such the Church appears like a company which services the religious interests of society or in certain cases represents a religious interest group within the religious market. It does not seem to be the way a whole people is invited to apprehend the call of God upon their lives. Thus these analogies are corrosive of the distinctive vocation, character and mission of the Church. Furthermore, such views imply that clear strategy and properly focused energy will deliver numerical growth, whereas existing practice will contribute to the ongoing decline of these 'religious companies'. It follows that responsibility for congregational decline is the responsibility of clergy and congregations who do not adhere to such a strategy, and this contributes further to depression among these clergy and congregations. Church growth becomes growth determined by human decision and is predominantly numerical growth since it can be quantified. In so doing, the survival of the Church is seen as a fundamentally human-centred project rather than the divinely led community envisaged by Hauerwas. This is despite the fact that the New Testament speaks little of church growth and more about God growing the Kingdom of Heaven.[11]

Hence many of the clergy I have visited, representing all Anglican traditions, are cautious about embracing approaches to church growth and mission which seem simply to be uncritical extensions of business, industrial, military or local government practice. In some way they are concerned that the identity of Church as a sign of the mission of God in the world needs to draw its shape and agenda from that mission and the character of God, rather than from practices which, though sometimes more efficient in building up attendance figures, are nevertheless rooted in a human calculus. In consequence they seem more at home with the story of Christian practice in Scripture and tradition that regards the Church as a mystical and divinely formed society rather than one which is primarily the result of human will. While mission in the world includes a functional dimension expressed in the commitment to love our neighbour, the Church's primary vocation is to worship and invite others to worship the God of Jesus Christ. Worship is the context in which God transforms or sanctifies congregations into signs of salvation. Consequently growing or developing the Church and directing its mission is primarily a divine responsibility. Human co-operation is required, but this is responsive and secondary to the divine missionary activity. In addition, the Church is a society being transformed by God on God's terms. As such it represents faith in flesh, a political community whose key missional significance lies in the character of its life together and the outworking of that life in evangelism, service and compassion. Brad Kallenberg calls this 'embodied apologetics' or the way the body of Christ is transformed into a rationale for the gospel.[12]

Mission as divine horticulture

Hauerwas's insights into character, community, narrative and performance, together with the insights of my clerical colleagues, suggest that God's way of mission has closer affinities with horticulture than with business, industry or the military. This is because the Church is better construed as an organism rather than an organization or indeed an institution. Of course, this is not to deny that there are elements of organization and institution in Church. Likewise strategy, leadership and management are possible in those aspects of its life, albeit in a carefully reflective way. It is worth noting that the New Testament locates leadership and management within a form of discipleship and ministry patterned on Christ's self-emptying in Philippians 2.5–11. In addition, the word for administration, *kubernesis*, used in 1 Corinthians 13.28, is a leadership word rooted in the imagery of a pilot or navigator carefully steering a boat at sea. It is, though, located amidst a range of other ministries that remind us that leadership is embedded and distributed in the Church and is one of a number of callings to enable the Church to flourish and grow as a body of disciples actively participating in the great epic of God's salvation. Organization and institution are important, but they are not the Church's primary identity. As a living organism the mission, ministry, growth and development of the Church are primarily facilitated by paying attention to the character of the organism and the conditions which favour its growth and development relative to its identity. This is because the possibilities for growth are predominantly present in the potential of the organism to grow under appropriate conditions. In terms of the Church, this potential is rooted in the creative life and activity of God. Human co-operation fosters the conditions for growth, just as paying attention to the soil, light, water, fertilizer and pests is necessary when growing plants. However, it is God who gives the growth, as Paul mentions in 1 Corinthians 3.6. As a result, what emerges bears the stamp of God's activity upon it and represents a contingent sign of salvation consistent with the wider mission of God.

Thus the Church is fundamentally a catholic organic community within which are many particular though related communities. It is not an institution or organization made up of broadly identical parts. Congregations are not franchised models of a single ideal akin to McDonald's outlets. Instead, they are contextual gatherings or mission stations of the catholic Church. Each congregation has its own distinctive vocation and identity within the mission of this wider Church, which lives within the mission of God. Hence any attempt to gauge the condition of a local church has to engage in an ethnographic approach which pays attention to the particular character of Church embodied in these differing dimensions.[13] As Helen Cameron remarks, 'congregations are diverse and not even those in the same denomination will share all characteristics in common'.[14] Yet in contemporary English society, shaped by the Enlightenment quest for abstraction and predictability, the Church is easily seduced into beginning with abstract systematic analysis which seems tidier, more efficient and predictable, rather than giving priority to the messy and often unsystematic character of its life as a community of storytellers.

The Church is primarily an organism rather than an institution or system, an embodied community rather than an abstract idea. Cultivating a missional Church is not about finding an ideal model of mission or system of church growth and then seeking to replicate or put into practice this ideal. Instead, it involves improvising upon the story of God carried in the Church's corporate memory within the horizon of the mission context of that particular embodiment of Church.[15] It is imaginatively exploring how to live as a holy community in a changing context. Thus mission, ministry, church growth and development benefit less from military metaphors of strategy and more from the horticultural metaphor of cultivation. Cultivating a missional Church involves paying attention to how conditions for mission are fostered within and around particular Christian communities rather than by imposing an abstract strategy claiming universal applicability. This sort of strategy presumes a hierarchical notion of powerful agents and compliant subordinates enabling those determining and implementing a strategy to require that it be effected in a 'top down' manner. This may be conceivable for an army or a company. It is more difficult to imagine in terms of very diverse and relatively independent congregations.

Cultivation recognizes that the power for life, growth and sharing lies fundamentally in the mystery of the organism and the conditions it is part of. As Paul comments, 'I planted, Apollos watered, but God gave the growth.'[16] Hence Kenyan roses cannot be forced to grow in Doncaster soil, however wonderful they may be. The key is to work the soil of Doncaster, ensure that light, fertilizer and water are present, and then let God work God's growth. Of course, local practice will draw upon wider experience as a way of fertilizing the immediate context. As in horticulture, it is possible to enrich the soil and improve conditions for growth using insights and resources discovered elsewhere, so long as they complement local wisdom. Nevertheless, it is sobering to read Paul Chambers' study into the destructive effects of ideological rather than interpretative approaches to ministry by two middle-class evangelical clergy serving consecutively in a conservative working-class parish in Wales. Their attempt to impose an abstract strategy for growth without consideration for the local congregation's history and disposition was disastrous. Similarly Matthew Guest's interesting insights into the way lay leaders rather than the clergy 'controlled' the ecclesial story of a large middle-class congregation in the north of England reveal the problems that emerge when vision and leadership are unreflectively parachuted into communities from outside.[17]

In the light of the above, statistics derived from across very diverse contexts have to be interpreted with caution. They may not tell us much about the faithfulness, appropriateness or indeed character of mission in particular contexts. At most they may invite reflection which can help illuminate and encourage appropriate mission in comparable contexts.[18] However, cultivation requires that local knowledge will qualify more detached insights since it will be a thicker description of what is taking place.[19] Clergy, in particular, need to be cautious about coming to swift judgements about the mission, ministry and the challenges facing a particular congregation. It takes time to understand the peculiarities of this community or that. What God's call to mission means for this congregation or that emerges as Christians practise faith together in contrast to theories derived in the abstract, which particular communities try to put into practice.

Stories, as Hauerwas reminds us, are therefore the prerequisites for cultivating holy missional communities.[20] As Helen Cameron suggests, this narrative approach is about developing appropriate rather than standard ways of working with distinctive communities in order to avoid crushing the informal and particular and recognizing the provisional character of such analysis.[21] In consequence, the approach is hermeneutical; that is, listening to and interpreting stories with a view to enabling disciples, parishes and ministers to grow in faith and service, rather than conforming them to abstract theories of discipleship, parish and ministerial development. It has affinities with spiritual direction.

Conclusion

Hauerwas's emphasis upon character, community, narrative and performance reminds us that cultivating holy missional communities is an art which involves co-operating with the Spirit who blows in mysterious and surprising ways. It is about co-operating with the Spirit to enable signs of salvation to grow, evangelistic signs which embody the grace of God and represent faith in flesh. The metaphor of cultivation underwrites the implication of common worship – namely that God is the primary agent in redemption and that missional communities are cultivated principally on divine terms through the effects of grace mediated in worship. Holiness in the Church is fundamentally divinely scribed rather than humanly scripted and thereby represents a divine signature in contemporary life. In short, it involves Spirit-inspired sanctification, whose cultivation includes human co-operation, but which is not determined by it. Such sanctification is not only the pre-requisite for effective mission, but is the condition whereby that mission is discerned, since it is as communities share in God's holiness through worship that they are formed to see what God is asking of them. Such worshipful attention includes learning the ways of God from other Christian communities, past and present. It also challenges congregations to recognize divinely informed wisdom beyond the Church, since the reign of God is not contained in the Church.

Questions

- In what ways does Hauerwas's work on character, community, narrative and performance make you think in fresh ways about the mission of your church?
- Why do you think Christians might be tempted by approaches to mission which franchise a 'successful' model?
- What sort of soil is your church planted in, and how could this soil be fertilized for the gospel?
- What is the relationship between worship and mission?

Notes

1 This represents a revised version of a paper published in *Crucible* (April 2007) and first given to the Church of England's Ministry Development Officer Network in March 2005, and later at the Diocesan Ministry Development Officers Conference held in the Diocese of Newcastle, Australia, in May 2006. For further reflections see John B. Thomson, *Church on Edge? Practising Christian Ministry Today*, London: Darton, Longman & Todd, 2004.

2 Stanley Hauerwas with Richard Bondi and David B. Burrell, *Truthfulness and Tragedy: Further Investigations into Christian Ethics*, 2nd edn, Notre Dame: University of Notre Dame Press, 1985, pp. 15–39.

3 *Truthfulness and Tragedy*, pp. 19–20.

4 *Truthfulness and Tragedy*, p. 21.

5 *Truthfulness and Tragedy*, p. 21.

6 See also Alasdair MacIntyre, *After Virtue*, 2nd edn, Notre Dame: University of Notre Dame Press, 1984, and *Whose Justice, Whose Rationality*, London: Duckworth, 1988, for a similar thesis.

7 Thus while recognizing the force of John Hull's challenge to the Church of England *Mission-Shaped Church* report, London: Church House Publishing, 2003, I remain persuaded that we discern the mission of God by actively participating in the public worship of the Christian community. Only through such transformation will our eyesight and hearing be attuned to the signs of the mission of God or God's Kingdom in the world. See John M. Hull, *Mission-Shaped Church: A Theological Response*, London: SCM, 2006, especially p. 31.

8 See Peter Collins, 'Congregations, Narrative and Identity: A Quaker Case Study', in Matthew Guest, Karin Tusting and Linda Woodhead (eds), *Congregational Studies in the UK: Christianity in a Post-Christian Context*, Aldershot: Ashgate, 2005, pp. 99–112.

9 Nicholas Lash, *Holiness and Silence: Reflections on the Question of God*, Aldershot: Ashgate, 2004, p. 43.

10 This approach is also advocated in Hans-Georg Gadamer, *Truth and Method*, 2nd edn, London: Sheed & Ward, 1993.

11 I am grateful for this insight to the Dean of Sheffield, Peter Bradley.

12 Brad J. Kallenberg, *Ethics as Grammar: Changing the Postmodern Subject*, Notre Dame: University of Notre Dame Press, 2001, p. 156.

13 See Timothy Jenkins, 'Congregational Cultures and the Boundaries of Identity', in *Congregational Studies in the UK*, pp. 113–21, where he argues that metropolitan abstract interpretations of a working-class congregation and its context completely misunderstand the dynamics of the situation and colonize the narrative with their own modernist interpretations. For a fuller account see Timothy Jenkins, *Religion in English Everyday Life: An Ethnographic Approach*, Oxford: Berghahn Books, 1999.

14 Helen Cameron, 'Are Congregations Associations?', in *Congregational Studies in the UK*, p. 148.

15 Samuel Wells, *Improvisation: The Drama of Christian Ethics*, London: SPCK, 2004.

16 1 Corinthians 3.6.

17 See Paul Chambers, 'The Effects of Evangelical Renewal on Mainstream Congregational Identities: A Welsh Case Study', and Matthew Guest, 'Friendship, Fellowship and Acceptance: The Public Discourse of a Thriving Evangelical Congregation', in *Congregational Studies in the UK*, pp. 57–69 and 71–84.

18 Lynda Barley's booklet shows the limitations of statistics for evaluating the success or failure of the Church. See Lynda Barley, *Churchgoing Today*, London: Church House Publishing, 2006.

19 Bob Jackson, *Hope for the Church: Contemporary Strategies for Growth*, London: Church House Publishing, 2002, and *The Road to Growth: Towards a Thriving Church*, London: Church House Publishing, 2005.

20 For earthed stories of churches engaged in mission see Susan Hope, *Mission-Shaped Spirituality*, London: Church House Publishing, 2006.

21 Cameron, in *Congregational Studies in the UK*, p. 149.

9

Witnessing Holiness[1]

> The principal themes from Hauerwas which inform this reflection are drawn from the following collections: *A Community of Character Toward a Constructive Christian Social Ethic*; *Christian Existence Today: Essays on Church, World and Living in Between*; *Dispatches from the Front: Theological Engagements with the Secular*; *Sanctify Them in the Truth: Holiness Exemplified*; *A Better Hope: Resources for a Church Confronting Capitalism*; *Democracy and Postmodernity*; and *Performing the Faith: Bonhoeffer and the Practice of Nonviolence.*

Introduction

My wife's family are from Morpeth near Newcastle in England. I am half Scottish. Yet remarkably, friendship and love have flourished between a Jacobite like myself and my wife's Geordie relatives. Indeed, this is all the more remarkable since traditionally our ancestors might well have been thieving bandits raiding each other's cattle across the border between Scotland and England, or indeed outlaws fleeing from our respective law-enforcing authorities. If we had been married in the seventeenth century, my wife and I would probably have been hanged by one or other side as traitors. In this chapter I want to reflect upon another remarkable phenomenon, the witness of the Church in late modern societies. To many, it does not seem remarkable at all, indeed quite the reverse. However, using the insights of Hauerwas, I hope to show that it has a remarkable character analogous to prickly pears in an African desert. Prickly pears are those uncomfortable yet life-sustaining fruit of the cactus which look so unappealing, yet witness to and resource life in the desert. Churches, like prickly pears, bear witness to the immanent life of God in the arid context of late modern societies by their presence, through practising their way of life and by sharing their story. As such they are fragile, often broken but nevertheless genuine signs of God's grace. Such signs offer material resources for Christian witness and indeed theology and thereby represent the pre-requisite for re-engaging late modern cultures with the gospel.

Practising theology

Brad Kallenberg has described the project of the American theological ethicist, Stanley Hauerwas, as an exercise in embodied apologetics.[2] According to Kallenberg, Hauerwas argues that the Church's calling in pluralist late modern societies is not to capitulate to contemporary ideals or try to reinvent itself to be relevant, but simply to become visibly more itself. That means that its primary vocation is to explore and live its identity, an identity into which it is formed as it gathers for worship. This divine formation generates an embodied apologetic, which is a tangible rationale for the plausibility of faith in God expressed in the way the Church lives and testifies. Hauerwas's project is therefore an attempt to recover the distinctive calling of the Christian community as a witness to God's activity in the world. Such a recovery depends upon the proper formation of the Church which happens as Christians perform ecclesial practices such as praying, confessing sins, listening to Scripture and participating in the sacraments. These train Christians to see and speak in the world as Christians.[3] Faith is formed through material practices, the communal activities Christians perform together as Christians. The challenge for the Church in late modern societies is to become a community whose life together embodies sufficient of the story of God to act both as an attraction and a challenge to those societies. This, though, is a peaceable rather than a manipulative witness. Unlike much church growth thinking, Hauerwas's approach suggests that the Church will not fulfil its vocation by marketing its ideology/faith correctly or in a way determined by the concerns of that society but by becoming more faithful and fluent practitioners of the faith through attention to God in worship. Thereby churches will witness to the character of God as they let God form them into such witnesses.

The truthful character of Christian performance is not primarily dependent upon human agency, though co-operation is required. Rather, it is underwritten by the active participation of God in the Church, since Immanuel, God-with-us, refuses to be absent when people gather in his name.[4] It is God's involvement among his people which enables the Church in its diverse and broken manifestations still to represent a social polity whereby Jesus is known to us today.[5] The Church does not justify itself, since God justifies it. It simply lives in trust that God will sustain its life and enable it to witness. Consequently Christian theologians are servants of the Church whose calling is to 'help Christians discover that the practices as common as praying for the sick during common worship have implications that are as wonderful as they are frightening'.[6] In late modern societies focused around the healthy autonomous self, the sick are strangers, outsiders, disturbances who speak about finitude and tragedy. Yet tragedy reminds us that we are not in complete control of our lives and thus finitude and fallibility invite us to consider the possibility of God.

Christian witness is rooted in who and what a community is and how it lives rather than in the clarity of its members' conceptual beliefs. It is about the practices of the body. According to Hauerwas, if Christian theology is to be truthful it needs to be 'embedded in the practices of actually lived communities'.[7] Otherwise theology may simply appear as another interesting but not arresting series of ideas. Such ideas may engage some, but many in late modern societies are suspicious of ideas and rhetoric, regarding them as manipulative power bids. This suspicion is more difficult to sustain when confronted by Christian communities whose lives are congruent with the divine story their tradition speaks of and whose identity signifies something of the universal appeal of that story.

Christian communities: divine signatures

One of the privileges of my present peripatetic role is sharing in worship with a range of congregations around South Yorkshire and the East Riding. Some are very fragile congregations, while others seem robust. However, the tenacity and commitment of those involved always surprises me. Their presence and walk with God, particularly in their weakness, illustrates the grace of God active among them. In a society overwhelmed by consumerism and self-referential choices, such congregations bear witness to the prior claim of God upon our lives and to the challenge of the story of Christ. By living faithfully before God as holy communities, such churches are formed into embryonic icons of Christ for the world. Thereby they represent divine signatures giving reason for faith in the living God active in contemporary society. Similarly, I have childhood memories of African Christians displaying a sometimes inarticulate theological witness, which scripted these Christians to resist corruption, alcohol abuse, casual sexual practices and even the tyrannical regime of Idi Amin. For some, such as Ugandan Archbishop Janani Luwum, this witness was at the cost of their lives. It also enabled Christians to bridge enormous social and racial divides, as seen in the mid-twentieth-century Balokole movement spawned by the East African Revival. In particular, the practices of communal confession and repentance evoked by the challenge to 'walk in the light' together as Christian community, were critical to the social character of that witness. These performances exhibited an engaging and challenging witness of the sort Hauerwas invites the wider Church to embrace. They are tangible expressions of 'God-with-us' illuminating and being illuminated by the Gospel stories.

Discipleship and theology

Such social discipleship, however, is not about putting into practice theories generated by academic theology. Rather, as Hauerwas has suggested, it is discovering that worshipping the sort of God revealed in Jesus Christ through Spirit, liturgy and Scripture forms people into a particular sort of community. In short, it is about contextual sanctification or inhabiting and embodying God's story in a particular place, a way of discipleship brought home to me during my experience as a priest and theological educator in South Africa.[8] Here inherited church doctrines were interrogated as worship and discipleship called into question the theological legitimacy of apartheid. Indeed, it was the transformation of people's sense of their worth before God discovered in the practices of worship, attention to Scripture and the surprising discovery that blacks and whites could be friends in Christ across racial divides and among themselves, which exposed the falsity of apartheid theology and its embodiment in the Dutch Reformed Church. In consequence we had an Afrikaner ex-South Africa Defence Force sergeant training for ordination at the Anglican seminary not simply among black folk but even more amazingly among the English-speaking descendants of those who interred his ancestors in concentration camps during the Anglo-Boer war.

Practice tested and developed this sort of sanctified theology. Indeed, it was the theology of practitioners in mission whose activities and energies left little time for formal reflection. Church leaders such as Archbishop Tutu, Alan Boesak, Frank Chikane, Gabriel Setiloane, Sigqibo Dwane and Stanley Magoba found that much of their time and energies were taken up performing the faith rather than writing systematic theological treatises. Any writing they did tended to be occasionalistic in the form of sermons and short lectures or papers: a theology 'on the hoof' reflective of the dynamic they were a part of.[9] This is not to say that Christian academics were not engaged in the struggle against apartheid, as John de Gruchy and Itumeleng and Bernadette Mosala, among others, indicate. However, the driving energy was not in the academy but in the Church, not in speculation but in embodied action. Indeed, as John de Gruchy makes clear, the theological agenda of the academy, provoked in the 1980s–early 1990s by this ecclesial struggle, was an attempt to articulate the theological meaning of the Church. It focused upon ecclesiology, the nature, mission and unity of the Church.[10] As a result a more catholic-embodied apologetics challenged the more sectarian apologetics of white Dutch Reformed Theology. This enfleshed catholicity illustrated the universal extent of God's salvation expressed in Christ and acted as a crucial indicator of theological truthfulness. This was a reminder that not all ecclesial embodiments offer a truthful apologetic for the gospel. As embodied sectarianism, Dutch Reformed Theology explicitly undermined the sign of God's universal salvation and was consequently rejected by the majority Church.

Embodied apologetics and contemporary theology

Two contemporary Anglican theologians, John Milbank and Rowan Williams, also recognize the relationship between embodied apologetics and theology. Like Hauerwas, they do their theology by reflecting upon the witness of the Church, past and present. Though their projects are distinctively different and include significant disagreements about the theological meaning of the Christian tradition, they share a commitment to root their theological projects in the practices and performance of the historic and contemporary Christian community rather than in abstract texts or ideas. It is through reflection upon the former that they distil theological insights which articulate Christian convictions about the ways of God with the world. Milbank's radical orthodoxy can be seen as a form of theological therapy, seeking to heal the Church from the pathology of late modernism.[11] He traces this pathology back to the divorce between God's will and God's identity proposed by the fourteenth-century nominalist theologians Duns Scotus and William of Occam. This led to the loss of a connection between Christian virtue and Christian politics or worship and ethics which allowed a form of secularism to emerge which had no need to learn its ethics through worship, theological formation and reflection. Yet for Milbank this secularism has become a form of nihilism. Its story of the cosmos and human life is ultimately about nothingness and emptiness and is corrosive of human flourishing.

Milbank's challenge to the Church is to re-inhabit its narrative or story of God in order to reconnect worship and ethics and thereby live this story of God's universal love and peace more faithfully. A recovery from the tradition of Augustine's doctrine of divine participation restores the worshipping Church to its place as a focal resource for re-imagining Christian witness. Indeed, this witness is intensified as diverse people across time and the world worship the true God and in this worship are transformed or divinized into the sign of God's salvation, a universal community gathered in Christ's name. Consequently belief is not primarily a set of ideas but the way a Christian community lives within the divine story. This liturgically and sacramentally formed way of life expresses an apologetic which Milbank expects to display something of the 'harmonious peaceable difference' of the life of the Trinity.

Rowan Williams' insights about the third-century Arian controversy over Christ's divinity display a similar attention to the character of the Church as providing material evidence for the saving activity of God in the world.[12] For Williams, Athanasius triumphed over Arius not because he had a more convincing grasp of biblical texts or indeed that his formal theological vision was beyond critique. What trumped Arius was the witness of the third-century Constantinian 'world' Church. Here was a provisional sign of universal community, a witness that God was in Christ redeeming the world. In Williams' interpretation of Athanasius' theology only God could ensure universal salvation. Human agency was too finite. Thus this dispute was fundamentally about the theological significance of the Church. For Athanasius, the sign of the Church at Nicea offered material support for the doctrines of Christ's divinity and of the Trinity. Hence theology begins with the practices and language of the Christian community, past and present. The Church performs its faith, and although the true meaning of Scripture and the Church's story awaits the disclosure of the *parousia*, the provisional, contextual and contingent manifestations of this story are signs of the divine story at work in the world.[13] For example, as the Church gathers and offers the Eucharist, meaningful flesh is constituted, that is flesh imbued with meaning, which invites others to engage and interpret that meaning or embodied apologetic.[14] Congregations are icons of Christ, which together contribute to the way God is understood in life. They may represent an ambiguous embodied apologetic, a broken icon. Nevertheless, they are God's new human race in embryo form, prickly pears speaking of paradise by witnessing to God's saving life in often arid conditions.

Conclusion

Hauerwas helps us to see that Christian theology is inextricably wedded to the material witness of the Church. How the Church performs and has performed the faith offers a more or less convincing theological rationale for the Christian story. An apologetic can be corrosive of that story if it embodies a form of life which undermines the character of that story, as Afrikaner theology has demonstrated. On the other hand, Christian communities seeking to live faithfully within that story offer material reason for others to take seriously the claims and possibilities that story speaks of. As mentioned above, in cultures characterized by suspicion about rhetoric and ideas, such material witness is of critical importance in mission. This is not so much about a new way of being Church, but rather is about faithful discipleship enabling God's grace to transform a community into a compelling witness for the gospel. Such living holiness is the potential gift of every congregation to those it is called to witness among.

Ordinary congregations engaged in fairly traditional ministry with all their limitations represent a powerful witness to the grace of God. Like Hauerwas, Milbank and Williams have also shown us that Christian communities performing basic discipleship practices embody theological truths and foster fruitful mission in late modern societies. These performances will be shaped by the training they receive as they worship together, since public worship trains Christians to be disciples and forms them to live as signs or icons of God's grace in their daily lives. Such performances embody theological claims about the character and salvation of God, which invite others to respond to this salvation. They remind us of the pivotal role of ordinary congregations in the mission of God and of the theological riches they witness to.

Questions

- What do you understand by the phrase 'embodied apologetics'?
- What is the relationship between the Church and theology?
- How can you distinguish between truthful and deceptive theology?
- In what ways do Christian practices inform the witness of your church?

Notes

1 A version of this chapter was given as the Morpeth Lecture 2006 in Newcastle, Australia. The Morpeth Lecture is jointly sponsored by the Diocese and the University of Newcastle, Australia.

2 Brad J. Kallenberg, *Ethics as Grammar: Changing the Postmodern Subject*, Notre Dame: University of Notre Dame Press, 2001, p. 156.

3 For the fullest exposition of Christian practices by Hauerwas, see *In Good Company: The Church as Polis*, Notre Dame: University of Notre Dame Press, 1995, pp. 153–68.

4 *Sanctify Them in the Truth: Holiness Exemplified*, Edinburgh: T. & T. Clark, 1998, pp. 6–7.

5 *A Community of Character: Toward a Constructive Christian Social Ethic*, 4th edn, Notre Dame: University of Notre Dame Press, 1986, p. 37.

6 *Sanctify Them*, p. 7.

7 *Sanctify Them*, p. 157.

8 John B. Thomson, 'Modern Christian Thought: South Africa', in Alistair McGrath, *Blackwell's Encyclopedia of Modern Theology*, Oxford: Blackwell, 1993, pp. 520–4.

9 See, for example, the contributions to Itumeleng Mosala and Buti Thlagale (eds), *The Unquestionable Right to be Free*, Johannesburg: Skotaville, 1986.

10 J. W. de Gruchy, 'South African Theology Comes of Age', *Religious Studies Review*, 17/3, July 1991.

11 For Milbank's thought, see John Milbank, *Theology and Social Theory: Beyond Secular Reason*, Oxford: Blackwell, 1990, *The Word Made Strange: Theology, Language, Culture*, Oxford: Blackwell, 1997, *Being Reconciled: Ontology and Pardon*, London: Routledge, 2003, and *The Future of Love: Essays in Political Theology*, London: SCM, 2009. For an introduction to Radical Orthodoxy, see Jeremy Morris (ed.), *Faith and Freedom: Exploring Radical Orthodoxy, Affirming Catholicism*, Third Millennium, 2003, and John Milbank, Catherine Pickstock and Graham Ward (eds), *Radical Orthodoxy: A New Theology*, London and New York: Routledge, 1999.

12 Rowan Williams, *Arius: Heresy and Tradition*, London: SCM, 2001, pp 234–9. See also Mike Higton, *Difficult Gospel: The Theology of Rowan Williams*, London: SCM, 2004, pp. 42–3.

13 Rowan Williams, *On Christian Theology*, Oxford: Blackwell, 2000, pp. 44–59, 167–80.

14 Rowan Williams, *Anglican Identities*, London: Darton, Longman & Todd, 2004, pp. 87–101.

10

Living Holiness

Living holiness in abstract societies

In previous chapters I have tried to explore Hauerwas's work on the Church and show its fruitfulness for ordinary Christian congregations, discipleship, ministry and mission. In conclusion, I want to suggest a number of ways in which his insights can help Christians negotiate the challenges of living in late modern societies within the North Atlantic context. A fundamental characteristic of this context is abstraction. The philosopher John Gray roots this disposition in the utopian thinking that sprang out of the rejection of Augustinian Christianity in the Enlightenment. This spawned the secular, though effectively religious, political quest to perfect human life.[1] The sociologist Charles Taylor locates it in the buffered self which emerged as the legacy of the Enlightenment. This modern self was disengaged, detached and individuated from all outside itself in sharp contrast to the porous social self of pre-modern times. The effect of this was to privilege freedom over virtue, legal rights over relational duties, social systems over communal identities, and gave rise to impersonal concepts such as 'the people' and 'equality'. As we have noted, this disposition was reinforced by the apparent objectivity, or positivism, of the natural sciences which seduced individual thinkers into imagining that they were detached spectators with a universally valid total picture of reality who could answer theodicy questions with confidence. In short, it represents a self-centred and excarnational approach to life in contrast to traditional Christianity's emphasis on incarnation and participation.[2]

It is the intrinsically abstract character of late modern societies that led the theologian John Milbank to claim that in these societies 'only Christianity fully celebrates the concrete and bodily'.[3] Despite lots of superficial talk about bodies and the importance of the material, much contemporary western life actually prefers abstractions to the messy details of human identity and living. For example, we are more frequently described as story-less types, collectives and individuals rather than families, communities and persons with particular stories that give our lives meaning. In society, the nation state now feels more state than nation as bureaucratization rather than a shared narrative forms the social glue of society. In Britain, politicians are increasingly worried that our sense of belonging is diminishing because we do not share an awareness of a common history. Passports and National Insurance numbers are all that label us British.

As a conclusion to this book, therefore, I want to reflect upon the context within which Hauerwas invites Christians to embody the story of God's grace. My argument is that, although we have benefited in many areas from technological and scientific developments, our human life-world, or the world of human flourishing, has been severely diminished due to a preoccupation with ideas and abstractions at the expense of such embodiment. Furthermore, it is this faith in the 'spirit' rather than the 'material' that has dislocated these societies from their Christian roots, although it is sobering to realize that major responsibility for the abstracting of late modern societies may well lie with elements of the Christian tradition itself. According to Charles Taylor, Christians of a more activist and reformist disposition lost touch with the practices and embodied character of ordinary church living in their enthusiasm to generate an ideal form of discipleship often called beliefs. This led to an excarnational rather than an incarnational approach to faith and contributed to the abstract character of North Atlantic societies as the latter became increasingly secularized and dis-embedded from any liturgical moorings.[4] The idealist drive neglected the particulars of context and people in a way that not only enabled the Enlightenment philosophers to imagine the objective spectator perspective but also contributed to the secularization of these societies as ordinary people gave up on the quest to become ideal. Although Hauerwas has sometimes been unfairly criticized as unrealistic, his project actually deconstructs this abstract idealism by rooting discipleship in the particular enfleshed practices of particular gatherings of Christians within the framework of time and place. Hauerwas seeks a transformed Church but not an idealistic one. Transformation is about becoming a variegated and material witness to God's grace in diverse contexts rather than a singular sign. There is nothing abstract about Hauerwas's Church, which makes this Church vital if Christians are to be faithful witnesses within highly abstract North Atlantic societies. His Church is faith in flesh, in sharp contrast to the faith in spirit prevalent in these societies.

Faith in spirit: consumerism

One example of this faith in spirit is consumerism evident in the contemporary obsession with shopping. Shopping has always been around and is important, economically and socially. However, in the recent past it has changed from being predominantly a means of obtaining the necessities and occasional luxuries of life to a total way of life. It is increasingly about defining one's identity through symbols of consumption and display, about purchasing a fantasy rather than embracing the details of one's own reality. As a result, shopping becomes bound up with belonging to a generalization rather than recognizing oneself as someone particular. In the past, belonging was configured around blood, baptism and battle. While each of these solidarities – and battle in particular – remains attractive to fragmented liberal societies seeking cohesion, the soft power of buying represents an even more seductive option. As Timothy Radcliffe comments,

> all human societies have markets, the buying and selling of goods. Western society differs in *being* a market. It is the fundamental model that dominates and forms our conception of society, politics and even of each other. Everything is for sale.[5]

Yet, as Barry Schwartz indicates in *The Paradox of Choice*, such consumerism, symbolized by ubiquitous shopping malls, fails to deliver long-term satisfaction as the pleasure of particular purchases is constantly subverted by the dream of a better future product.[6] The fantasy therefore proves elusive and the dream of escaping the messy reality of our lives is regularly thwarted. The shopping experience, though exciting in the short term, therefore ultimately disappoints and generates a sense of emptiness. Furthermore, this emptiness intensifies since the formal availability of everything means that nothing is particularly special, which itself makes our choosing seem arbitrary. In addition, every particular choice brings with it a tranche of opportunity costs relating to the potential alternatives available. These abstract opportunity costs weigh down heavily upon us, denying us the pleasure of our actual choice by rendering it relative to all the other formal choices we might have made.

With so many possibilities and no simple criteria for choice, we feel desperate to 'get it right' yet lack confidence in our judgements, particularly when these are constantly called into question by the power of advertising.[7] Buyers' remorse is intensified as the possibilities we have not purchased challenge the value of what we have actually bought. Equally, the thrill of buying increasingly delivers less as frequent shopping makes each choice less significant relative to all the others. Furthermore, colonized by the cloning pressures of marketing and fashion, our real bodies are constantly being criticized by the ideal fantasies of the visual media. Paradoxically, for all the flesh on display, such advertising promotes ideals we can never be.

As we have seen, Hauerwas's answer to consumerism is the Church. His most explicit engagement with the theme is in the collection *A Better Hope: Resources for a Church Confronting Capitalism, Democracy and Postmodernity*. In these essays he deconstructs the effects of North American capitalism as a false description of life which subverts substantial identities in its quest for fluidity, ephemeral relationships and consumption.[8] Yet his response is not to outline a series of rules or abstract models for Christian living but instead to point to the Church's formative practices. They will form Christians to recognize their fundamental identity as the Church and thereby know how to shop faithfully. These practices are focused in worship which 'is the practice that sums up or gives direction to all we do as Christians. It is the fundamental performance of faith that, for example, shapes what we talk about and how we talk as Christians.'[9] For example, Christian talk will describe care for and conversation with the elderly as vital to the health of the Church and society. Indeed, it will hold elderly disciples morally responsible for transmitting their wisdom so that the young can begin to deal fruitfully with the realities of finitude, ageing, memory, time, sickness and tragedy.[10] In this way they will enable people of all ages to remain productive and thereby resist the consumer myth of late modern capitalism that we can produce nothing.[11] The elderly also remind the young that the past matters since the abstract, traditionless chooser formed by late modern capitalism is prey to the manipulative powers present in media and economics. Only as agents consciously rooted and formed in an intergenerational community with a truthful story can the young be equipped to choose discriminatingly and faithfully and consume wisely.[12] Without such rootedness and formation they are simply swamped by the overwhelming power of late modern capitalism. This calls to mind the impotence of a figure such as Albert Speer, the German technocrat who executed Hitler's orders without question because he had no substantial story within which to understand his vocation. Young Christians, on the other hand, will become aware of their primary Christian narrative identity and thereby be equipped with the resources to resist being colonized by the abstractions of consumerism.[13]

Faith in spirit: state

Second, the state is becoming more abstract as globalization diminishes the power of the nation state, even taking account of the emergency activity of the state consequent upon the recent collapse of international free market capitalism. According to Philip Bobbitt, western states are now effectively market states; that is, states that can at best offer their citizens the formal capacities to flourish in the brave new world of the world market, but which increasingly cannot offer the tangible benefits of social security, national security and self-conscious ethnic identity/history.[14] Hence the state, already something of an abstraction, is increasingly divorced from the lives of those it purports to represent. Without a sense of embodying its people, the market state becomes a site of alienation, with large numbers of its 'citizens' disassociating themselves from its procedures. Hence, on the one hand, as 'citizens', many no longer bother to vote or participate in public life. On the other hand, as consumers, they increasingly demand more from the state in terms of health, education and other welfare provision at the very time when it cannot deliver. Loyalty to the nation state, the engine of resistance to Nazism in World War Two, is now a concept alien to many. Furthermore, as Anthony Giddens comments, 'Modern institutions differ from all preceding forms of social order in respect of their dynamism, the degree to which they undercut traditional habits and customs, and their global impact.'[15] They therefore subvert loyalty to tangible communities by corroding the bonds that held those communities together. Contracts and collectives replace covenants and communities. Abstraction displaces the specificity of the flesh, generating a gulf between people and their societies. What seemed substantial again emerges as increasingly 'spiritual' or disembodied.

Once again Hauerwas's response to this abstraction is the Church. While his interpretation of Church–state relations in the European context may be contestable, he is correct in his view that the state needs the Church to challenge the temptation to hubris. The Church does this by embodying in its worship and politics an explicit attention to the divine story. Thus although John Gray contests the description of the United States as a market state, believing that its national interest has always taken priority, Hauerwas would argue that the market is indeed the national interest of a country whose religion is money. In contrast, the Church is a polity orientated through worship to see the world as more than a human playground. It represents a more substantial polity than the state, earthed as it is in devotional practices that prioritize tangible service rather than abstractions such as electronic markets.[16]

The story the Church narrates furthermore describes the cosmos as a divine gift within which the state is located and accountable. It also relativizes the nation state by reminding it that the Church is a greater and more catholic community representing a more realistic sign of the universal love and reach of God's grace. Yet in so doing, Hauerwas is not suggesting that Christians abdicate themselves from the socio-political realm. Certainly he is hostile to the Constantinianism of the medieval settlement and even more so to the neo-Constantinianism of the nation state, because the latter reduces the Church to a servant of a particular society rather than witnessing as a Church across the nations to the universal reign of God. However, he does believe that Christians can engage tactically within that state so long as their actions are under the rule of Christ because the contemporary state is in part the legacy of Christian mission.[17] Nevertheless, he is critical of Christians who uncritically embrace the rhetoric of the liberal state without reflecting carefully about its political ideas.[18] Concepts such as freedom, justice, the Christian nation, democracy and indeed liberation can easily mask views of human identity which are corrosive to the Church.[19] Indeed,

> the inability of the Protestant churches in America to maintain any sense of authority over the lives of their members is one of the most compelling signs that freedom of religion has resulted in the corruption of Christians, who now believe they have the right, religiously, to 'make up their minds'.[20]

These churches have failed to see that Christians are called to discipleship rather than an abstraction called 'freedom'. They have also colluded with consumer culture by reducing the Church to a religious product in a buyers' market. This forces churches to win customers through friendship, caring and lifestyle incentives rather than forming them, often painfully, in the practices which will enable them to embody the truth about God faithfully.

Furthermore, this preoccupation with freedom of choice corrupts practices such as Christian marriage and the family as these become emotively determined relationships rather than representing stable and social practices that embody Christian love for the next generation. 'The love required in marriage functions politically by defining the nature of Christian social order into which children and welcomed and trained.[21] In modernity, the nation state effectively takes the place of God, the Church and often the parent as it demands self-sacrifice through war, uses war as a form of social cohesion and imperial ambition, rivals the biological family in the nurture of the young, and treats all accountabilities except its own as voluntary. Hauerwas believes that in doing so it threatens the primary polity of the Church for Christians. For example, abstract slogans such as justice and peace are often presumed to be universally valid concepts, when Christians can only properly understand them through the narrative of the story of God.

This does not mean that Hauerwas rejects any involvement with the state. His own employment by a secular university and his thoughts on police work indicate a critical openness to such involvement. Police officers are officers of the state and are distinguished from soldiers because 'most of what police officers do is a non-violent response to violence. After all, police officers are called peace officers.'[22] Nevertheless, the Church's service to the state role will involve recounting truthful history about society to expose any deceptive story the state may tell about itself and others. Indeed, worship involves 'the ability to remember wrongs without them becoming occasions for self-justifying actions' and so breaks any revenge cycles rooted in past abuses.[23] In addition, the Church will embody a prophetic sign of Christ in its care for the unborn, children, the vulnerable and the elderly so that, as Enda McDonagh suggests, the Church becomes a divinely formed yet humble servant of the people.[24]

Faith in spirit: utopia

The ambition of the eighteenth-century Enlightenment was to achieve peace by ridding the world of religious controversy and replacing it with a single agreed language which could describe, understand and explain the totality of the universe. In this way it was believed that ambiguous material signs would be replaced by clear, unequivocal rational ideas and the dream of social and political harmony be realized.[25] The bloodshed of the Wars of Religion together with the emerging natural sciences and possibilities for exploration disposed many in Europe to seek another way forward than confrontation caused by 'dogma'. Hauerwas notes that according to William Cavanaugh, this also provided a pretext for the new nation states to claim legitimacy for themselves as competing plural ideologies and changed 'religion' into abstract beliefs or ideas rather than the way of life of the international catholic Christian community. This consequently gave the new lay elites of these nation states the opportunity to establish their political and economic dominance using the rhetoric of freedom of religion.[26] Indeed, the United States of America represented, for its white population at least, an experiment in leaving behind the troublesome past and concentrating on forging a new future free from this past, a future in which the goal of human perfection or salvation could be achieved within history.[27] In short, the United States was the laboratory of the Enlightenment in a way even France, with its symbols of the *Ancien Régime*, could not achieve. By the late eighteenth century the United States had become an experiment in this new understanding of the world. Strictly speaking, immigrants 'forgot' their prior identity as they arrived in the United States and became 'Enlightenment people', memory-less, able to converse in a common tongue and encouraged to believe that they could realize any dreams they entertained by hard work and an optimistic attitude.

Interestingly it is from within this society that two conflicting interpretations of the late twentieth- and early twenty-first-century world order have emerged.[28] The first, Francis Fukuyama writing in the aftermath of the 1989 fall of the Berlin Wall and end of what Bobbitt calls the 'Long War', proclaimed the 'end of history' as a way of asserting that the Enlightenment experiment had triumphed over its rivals.[29] The world's dominant ideology was free and peaceable market economics. Henceforth all societies would eventually make their way towards this goal, led by the example of the United States of America. Ironically this utopian optimism legitimized the ambiguous interventionism of the Iraq war and the simplistic imperialistic ideals of neo-conservatism that underwrote it, since it assumed that there was no need to pay attention to the complex narratives of the past which continued to inform the identity and conditions of the contemporary Middle East. The second, Samuel Huntington, argued in contrast that far from ushering in an age of peace, the end of this 'Long War' actually engendered another potential conflict, which he called a 'clash of civilizations'. In this scenario, societies of the Enlightenment such as the United States and its allies could be pitted against a number of hostile fundamentalist constituencies, particularly militant Islam. Though evidently simplistic, since radical Islam is as hostile to traditional Muslim societies as it is to the west and indeed represents a mutation of modern fundamentalism rather than a purification of Islam, the attraction of the thesis lay in its binary view of the world.[30] Huntington believed that the danger of this conflict was the unwillingness of either side to understand the other since neither could see any possibility of dialogue. Both sides are utopians which cannot brook the existence of the other. Despite this temptation he suggested a pragmatic approach whereby the west seeks to understand rather than trample over the integrities of other civilizations so that the world will not descend into perpetual conflict. However, it is not clear whether either antagonist has the patience to undertake this, preferring conflict to the time-consuming character of peacemaking.[31]

These two thinkers paradoxically flag up the threat of post-Enlightenment utopianism. The first scenario sees the arrival of utopia through the collapse of diversity into singularity as the power of the free market dream wins through economically and socially. On this view the Berlin Wall collapsed as a result of the soft power of capitalism and not through military victory. The second scenario destroys difference through the military victory of one party over the other. Both theories describe attempts to realize a utopia through the triumph of a single ideology that can brook no rivals. Both involve the effective destruction of difference since neither of these two scenarios presents us with a world in which diversity is respected, the stranger embraced as a friend and the destructiveness of evil neutered through forgiveness. As Rabbi Jonathan Sachs argues, such utopian positions subvert the possibility of negotiating different perspectives and values through conversation and without requiring the diminishment or destruction of the other. Utopia is achieved through the destruction of difference. Yet unless different civilizations understand each other's distinctiveness and difference respectfully, the world will become a violent rather than a peaceful order.

Hauerwas would not be surprised by the intrinsic and central place of violence evident in the utopian dreams described by Fukuyama and Huntington. Both approaches to utopia are violent because they are rooted in a liberal view of human identity which radically abstracts and individuates human beings from any communal identity and thereby renders others as threats rather than friends. This contrasts with the Church, which Hauerwas characterizes as a community of friends who embody a way of living which reflects the tangible friendship of God. This friendship is all about faith in flesh rather than in abstract beliefs or ideas and is captured in the focal metaphor of the Church as the 'body of Christ'. Theologically the body of Christ has a fourfold expression: the historical body of Jesus, the ecclesial body of the baptized, the sacramental body of the Eucharist, and the glorified body of the ascended Christ. Each expression of this body represents the call to tangible holiness expressed in a fleshly community of diverse peoples held together through worship by grace.

Yet in presenting the Church as a contrast to utopian idealism, Hauerwas faces the ambiguous history of the Church which includes evidence of its own seduction by abstract, idealistic and violent utopias. His response is to direct us back to the practices of the Church which continually deconstruct such abstract, idealistic and violent temptations from within the Christian tradition. These practices, he believes, properly form a peaceable people, a catholic community within which difference is celebrated rather than crushed. This peaceableness is not a state but a process whereby God's holiness gradually and sometimes painfully shapes the holiness of the Church more into the divine likeness. It always has a provisional rather than a utopian character and consequently there will be disagreements about the possibilities and parameters of this peaceableness, as debates about just-war criteria and the meaning of Constantinian display. Nevertheless, giving the Peace in the Eucharist signifies both peace between God and the Church and the challenge to embody peace within the Church and beyond it. The very tangibility of this liturgical action and the requirement that it be performed in public act as checks on any tendencies to treat people violently by reducing them to abstractions or caricatures. Similarly the Dismissal at the end of the liturgy propels Christians into the world nourished by the peaceable meal so that they can inhabit the world peaceably. Liturgy trains disciples in the Christian virtues which enable them to embody the peace-making holiness of God in the contexts they find themselves caught up in.[32]

One such site which Hauerwas inhabits is the modern university. This has become a context for legitimizing and promoting the sort of utopian, idealistic and violent narratives about human possibilities underlying liberal thinking, despite the fact that liberalism is actually 'the story of freedom from reverence, fidelity, neighbourliness and stewardship' characterized by the breaking of fidelity and the making of divisions represented in adultery and divorce.[33] Given its drive to professionalism, specialization and a commitment to the new religion of progress, the university exposes 'the problem for Christians and non-Christians alike [which] is the Christian inability to live in a way that enables us to articulate what difference it makes that we are or are not Christian'.[34] Yet because the university is properly orientated to the pursuit of truth, the Church's own commitment to truthful living requires it to bear witness within this environment as a form of neighbourly love. Hauerwas, therefore, seeks to be part of a Church which produces theology that can speak in a Christian way to the university. He believes that this is only possible because of the embodied character of the Church which is rooted in local contexts and in the discipline of liturgical time. This enables the Church to contest the abstract and globalized fantasies of the modern university and the utopianism it represents because it continually confronts these fantasies with located flesh and blood. The Church is always somewhere, whereas utopias are literally nowhere.[35] It is among the poor rather than simply among the rich and powerful elites and embodies contingency rather than advocating timeless ideals. The Church therefore lives among the realities of life in such as way that its theology can articulate the Augustinian view of truth as the adequation of knowledge with the real.[36]

The Church also represents a way of engaging truthfully with God and the world that resists the spiritualizing of faith as a set of beliefs that can be held independently of participating in the life of that Church. It does this by integrating the development of virtue and memory with the acquisition of knowledge and wisdom. This is in contrast to the liberal thinking dominant in the contemporary university which regards such formation as inhibiting human freedom and yet is effectively controlled by money. The Church therefore has to remind the university about its origins in the communal and formative integration of prayer and learning in the monasteries. It also challenges Christians who work in this context to re-inhabit the contemporary ruins of the university with a view to re-establishing a civilization of love rather than accepting the policed and violent ideas of liberalism.[37] This means that Hauerwas wants the university to be a genuinely plural context for learning rather than one whose inclusivity masks a hidden form of American universalism that has no space for real difference. Such a context can be fostered if Christian academics engage in non-coercive conversations with other specialists in ways which take account of context, occasion and contingency and avoid abstractions. In this way the driver for truthful research will be friendship rather than money and the universalist spectator perspective will be rejected in favour of local and particular ones.[38] Furthermore, this will begin to counter the subversive effect of capitalism which conflates the citizen and consumer into abstract, traditionless and impotent choosers and the dominant narrative of the homeless or utopian intellectuals whose ideals the modern university espouses will no longer be imposed upon all.[39]

Living holiness

Hauerwas's work offers a different perspective on the world.

- In place of dislocated, individuated and abstract identity, he sees in the fleshly Church a location for a stable and creative community of character, rooted in the epic story of God's ways with the world and expressed in the tangible practices of Christian discipleship.
- At a time when traditional forms of belonging, such as the biological family and the nation state, have been corroded by the effects of choice and globalization, he offers us a catholic Church within which all have a privileged place, and particularly the most vulnerable.
- In an era when peacemaking is usually the imposition of order by the powerful, he points us to a way of living configured around peaceableness, the respectful and careful invitation of friendship to strangers, which does not have to be successful according to the standards of the world because this peaceableness is the guaranteed destiny of the redeemed created order.
- When we are overwhelmed with ubiquitous consumerism and its fantasies, his project points us to a Church within which we are formed to make good judgements and choices.
- He reminds the Church that its freedom is a freedom for the service of God rather than a freedom from God.
- He reminds the Church that its agenda is to be Christ-centred rather than human-centred.

- He reminds the Church that its descriptive language emerges through its primary conversation with the God of Jesus Christ.
- He reminds the Church that it lives in the time God gives it to witness and express the divine hospitality of salvation.

I have tried to show that there are contemporary signs of the sort of Church that Hauerwas expects God to bring about. They are not powerful signs and they can easily be ridiculed. However, without the requirement to be a success these congregational signs can be faithful witnesses even in their fragility since it is common, corporate worship which generates their Christian ethic and gives them a language of testimony. Furthermore, this formation enables these communities to interpret and contribute competently and pertinently to the story of God focused in the Scriptures. Indeed, they best embody this story by becoming prophetic signs of the gospel in the diverse contexts they find themselves within. To this end, growth is about growing in holiness before it is about growing in numbers. The Church's growth must be intensive if it is to remain faithful in extensive growth, since the agency for growth is God's Spirit rather than human energy. The Church co-operates with the activity of God's Spirit through living holiness and sharing its story freely, imaginatively and generously. Christian communities thereby become divine signatures, indicating that the cosmos is not a void but a divinely treasured gift. This gift is recognized by the world as Christians perform their story and become an embodied apologetic for the gospel.

Hauerwas's work helps Christians to reflect deeply upon their vocation as Church in late modern societies. In these societies:

- The Church represents a distinctively Christian ethic within which disciples become agents witnessing to the story of God through faithful communal living holiness.[40]
- The Church embodies a peculiarly Christian rationality which assumes that the intelligibility of the cosmos is rooted in the story of God present in Christ and that the truthfulness of this divine story is displayed in its capacity to narrate tragedy

hopefully and to give time to the marginal and apparently insignificant.[41]

- The Church lives a story whose social ethics exposes the limits of liberal democracy and indicates the peaceable and servant reign of God present in the Church.[42]
- The Church's ethics are intrinsically theological, attentive to the importance of memory and committed to challenging the norm of war. They ensure that matters of life and death reflect both the gift of life and the importance of a good memory in death. Theodicy may be an expression of human hubris, but the challenge to it comes not from more theories about God and suffering, but through narratives that display how to suffer and die well in the hope of Christ.[43]
- The Church is becoming a prophetic sign with a public ministry ordered to keep this sign clear and faithful in the corrosive conditions of liberal societies.[44] To achieve this, the Church will need to re-learn how to read its Scriptures and to locate these Scriptures and its life within the great epic of God's story.[45] It will also need to become more aware of the extent of its Christian allies as well as being clear about the Christian character of the virtues and habits of its training so that these do not mask a violent pagan tradition under the guise of attractive rhetoric.[46]
- All of this will enable the Church to speak about and exemplify holiness as truth for the world through its peaceable performance of the practices of Christian discipleship.[47]

Hauerwas's work is not without its critics. However, I hope that this book reveals the fruitfulness of Hauerwas's work for ordinary Christian disciples and congregations, particularly at ground level. Hauerwas provides us with a way of being Church which is rooted in the faithfulness of God and focused in the witness of Christ which is now present in the Church. Such a witness has much to offer in late modern societies as a way of living holiness.

Questions

- In what ways might Hauerwas help your church to be a more faithful Christian community?
- Can you think of particular ways your church might enable Christians to resist the abstractions of modern life?
- What are the most significant insights you have gained from Hauerwas's work?

Notes

1 John Gray, *Black Mass: Apocalyptic Religion and the Death of Utopia*, London: Penguin Books, 2007. See also the Introduction in John Gray, *Gray's Anatomy: Selected Writings*, London: Alan Lane, 2009, pp. 1–17.

2 Charles Taylor, *A Secular Age*, Cambridge: Belknap Press, 2007, pp. 25–42, 159–75, 96–216, 288–90.

3 John Milbank, *Being Reconciled: Ontology and Pardon*, London: Routledge, 2003, p. 209.

4 Taylor, *A Secular Age*, pp. 288, 428–70 and 614–15.

5 Timothy Radcliffe, OP, *Sing a New Song: The Christian Vocation*, Dublin: Dominican Publications, 1999, p. 47.

6 Barry Schwartz, *The Paradox of Choice: Why More is Less*, New York: HarperCollins, 2004.

7 *The Paradox of Choice*, pp. 120–42.

8 *A Better Hope: Resources for a Church Confronting Capitalism, Democracy and Postmodernity*, Grand Rapids: Brazos Press, 2000, pp. 50–1.

9 *A Better Hope*, p. 19.

10 *A Better Hope*, pp. 173–88.

11 *A Better Hope*, p. 50.

12 *The State of the University: Academic Knowledge and the Knowledge of God*, Oxford: Blackwell, 2007, p. 149, footnote 12.

13 Stanley Hauerwas with Richard Bondi and David B. Burrell, *Truthfulness and Tragedy: Further Investigations into Christian Ethics*, 2nd edn, Notre Dame: University of Notre Dame Press, 1985, pp. 79–98.

14 Philip Bobbitt, *The Shield of Achilles: War, Peace and the Course of History*, London: Penguin Books, 2002, pp. 213–42.

15 Anthony Giddens, *Modernity and Self-Identity: Self and Society in the Late Modern Age*, Cambridge: Polity Press, 1991, p. 1.

16 See Gray, *Black Mass*, p. 255, and Hauerwas in *A Better Hope*, pp. 146–8.

17 *With the Grain of the Universe: The Church, Witness and Natural Theology*, Grand Rapids: Brazos Press, 2001, pp. 221–5.

18 See Stanley Hauerwas and William H. Willimon, *Resident Aliens: Life in the Christian Colony*, Nashville: Abingdon Press, 1989, for his comments to this end.

19 *After Christendom? How the Church is to Behave if Freedom, Justice and a Christian Nation are Bad Ideas*, Nashville: Abingdon, 1993, pp. 45–92.

20 *After Christendom*, p. 88.

21 *After Christendom*, p. 127.

22 *A Better Hope*, p. 208, footnote 19.

23 Charles T. Matthewes, 'Appreciating Hauerwas: One Hand Clapping', in *The Anglican Theological Review*, 82/2, 2000, p. 362.

24 Mark Thiessen Nation and Samuel Wells (eds), *Faithfulness and Fortitude: In Conversation with the Theological Ethics of Stanley Hauerwas*, Edinburgh: T. & T. Clark, 2000, pp. 17, 292–309.

25 See Gray, *Black Mass.*

26 William Cavannagh, *The Political Imagination*, Edinburgh: T. & T. Clark, 2002, quoted in *The State of the University*, pp. 60–5.

27 Gray, *Black Mass*, pp. 31 and 53.

28 Francis Fukuyama, *The End of History and the Last Man*, Harmondsworth: Penguin, 1992, and Samuel P. Huntington, *The Clash of Civilizations and the Remaking of World Order*, London: Touchstone, 1998.

29 Bobbitt, *The Shield of Achilles.*

30 Gray, *Black Mass*, pp. 168–9 and 251.

31 Huntington, *The Clash of Civilizations*, pp. 318–21.

32 See 'The Liturgical Shape of the Christian Life: Teaching Christian Ethics as Worship', in *In Good Company: The Church as Polis*, Notre Dame: University of Notre Dame Press, 1995, pp. 153–63.

33 *With the Grain of the Universe*, p. 233, footnote 61.

34 *With the Grain of the Universe*, p. 231.

35 *The State of the University*, pp. 3–8. See also *Christian Existence Today: Essays on Church, World and Living in Between*, Durham: The Labyrinth Press, 1988, pp. 221–52.

36 *The State of the University*, p. 22.

37 *The State of the University*, pp. 55–6.

38 *The State of the University*, pp. 94–100.

39 *The State of the University*, pp. 194–8.

40 See *A Community of Character: Toward a Constructive Christian Social Ethic*, 4th edn, Notre Dame: University of Notre Dame Press, 1986.

41 See *Truthfulness and Tragedy*.

42 See *A Community of Character* and *The Peaceable Kingdom: A Primer in Christian Ethics*, 3rd edn, Notre Dame and London: University of Notre Dame Press, 1986.

43 See *Against the Nations: War and Survival in a Liberal Society*, Notre Dame: University of Notre Dame Press, 1992, *Suffering Presence: Theological Reflections on Medicine, the Mentally Handicapped and the Church*, Edinburgh: T. & T. Clark, 1988, and *Naming the Silences: God, Medicine and the Problem of Suffering*, 2nd edn, Edinburgh: T. & T. Clark, 1993.

44 See *Christian Existence Today*.

45 See *Unleashing the Scriptures: Freeing the Bible from Captivity to America*, Nashville: Abingdon Press, 1993.

46 See *In Good Company*, and Stanley Hauerwas and Charles Pinches, *Christians Among the Virtues: Theological Conversations with Ancient and Modern Ethics*, Notre Dame: University of Notre Dame Press, 1997.

47 See *Sanctify Them in the Truth: Holiness Exemplified*, Edinburgh: T. & T. Clark, 1998, and *Performing the Faith: Bonhoeffer and the Practice of Nonviolence*, London: SPCK, 2004.

Select Bibliography

Allchin, A.M., *Participation in God: A Forgotten Strand in Anglican Tradition*, London: Darton, Longman & Todd, 1988.

Avis, Paul, *Ecumenical Theology and the Elusiveness of Doctrine*, London: SPCK, 1986.

—— *Anglicanism and the Christian Church: Theological Resources in Historical Perspective*, Edinburgh: T. & T. Clark, 1989.

—— *The Anglican Understanding of the Church: An Introduction*, London: SPCK, 2000.

Bartley, Jonathan, *Faith and Politics After Christendom: The Church as a Movement for Anarchy*, Milton Keynes: Paternoster, 2006.

Baukham, Richard (ed.), *God Will Be All in All: The Eschatology of Jürgen Moltmann*, Edinburgh: T. & T. Clark, 1999.

Bobbitt, Philip, *The Shield of Achilles: War, Peace and the Course of History*, London: Penguin Books, 2002.

Bradshaw, Timothy (ed.), *The Way Forward? Christian Voices on Homosexuality and the Church*, London: Hodder & Stoughton, 1997.

Checkland, Peter and Jim Scholes, *Soft Systems Methodology in Action*, New York: John Wiley & Sons, 1990.

Davie, Grace, *Religion in Britain Since 1945: Believing without Belonging*, Oxford: Oxford University Press, 1994.

—— *Europe: The Exceptional Case: Parameters of Faith in the Modern World*, London: Darton, Longman & Todd, 2002.

—— *The Sociology of Religion*, London: Sage, 2007.

Davie, Grace, Paul Heelas and Linda Woodhead (eds), *Predicting Religion: Christian, Secular and Alternative Futures*, Aldershot: Ashgate, 2003.

Frei, Hans, *The Eclipse of Biblical Narrative: A Study in Eighteenth and Nineteenth Century Hermeneutics*, New Haven and London: Yale University Press, 1974.

Fukuyama, Francis, *The End of History and the Last Man*, Harmondsworth: Penguin, 1992.

Gadamer, Hans-Georg, *Truth and Method*, 2nd edn, London: Sheed & Ward, 1993.

Gardner, Paul, Chris Wright and Chris Green (eds), *Fanning the Flame: Bible, Cross and Mission: Meeting the Challenge in a Changing World*, Grand Rapids, MI: Zondervan, 2003.

Giddens, Anthony, *Modernity and Self-Identity: Self and Society in the Late Modern Age*, Cambridge: Polity Press, 1991.

—— *The Third Way and Its Critics*, Cambridge: Polity Press, 2000.

Gill, Robin, *Churchgoing and Christian Ethics*, Cambridge: Cambridge University Press, 1999.

Gray, John, *Black Mass: Apocalyptic Religion and the Death of Utopia*, London: Penguin Books, 2007.

—— *Gray's Anatomy: Selected Writings*, London: Alan Lane, 2009.

Guest, Matthew, Karin Tusting and Linda Woodhead (eds), *Congregational Studies in the UK: Christianity in a Post-Christian Context*, Aldershot: Ashgate, 2005.

Hastings, Adrian, *The Construction of Nationhood: Ethnicity, Religion and Nationalism*, Cambridge: Cambridge University Press, 1997.

Hauerwas, Stanley, *Vision and Virtue: Essays in Christian Ethical Reflection*, Notre Dame: University of Notre Dame Press, 1981.

—— *A Community of Character: Toward a Constructive Christian Social Ethic*, 4th edn, Notre Dame: University of Notre Dame Press, 1986.

—— *The Peaceable Kingdom: A Primer in Christian Ethics*, 3rd edn, Notre Dame and London: University of Notre Dame Press, 1986.

—— *Christian Existence Today: Essays on Church, World and Living in Between*, Durham, NC: The Labyrinth Press, 1988.

—— *Suffering Presence: Theological Reflections on Medicine, the Mentally Handicapped and the Church*, Edinburgh: T. & T. Clark, 1988.

Hauerwas, Stanley, *After Christendom? How the Church is to Behave if Freedom, Justice and a Christian Nation are Bad Ideas*, Nashville: Abingdon Press, 1991.

—— *Against the Nations: War and Survival in a Liberal Society*, Notre Dame: University of Notre Dame Press, 1992.

—— *Unleashing the Scripture: Freeing the Bible from Captivity to America*, Nashville: Abingdon Press, 1993.

—— *Naming the Silences: God, Medicine and the Problem of Suffering*, 2nd edn, Edinburgh: T. & T. Clark, 1993.

—— *Dispatches from the Front: Theological Engagements with the Secular*, Durham, NC and London: Duke University Press, 1994.

—— *Character and the Christian Life: A Study in Christian Ethics*, 2nd edn, Notre Dame: University of Notre Dame Press, 1995.

—— *In Good Company: The Church as Polis*, Notre Dame: University of Notre Dame Press, 1995.

—— *Wilderness Wanderings: Probing Twentieth-Century Theology and Philosophy*, Boulder, CO: Westview Press, 1997.

—— *Sanctify Them in the Truth: Holiness Exemplified*, Edinburgh: T. & T. Clark, 1998.

—— *A Better Hope: Resources for a Church Confronting Capitalism, Democracy and Postmodernity*, Grand Rapids: Brazos Press, 2000.

—— *With the Grain of the Universe: The Church, Witness and Natural Theology*, Grand Rapids: Brazos Press, 2001.

—— *Performing the Faith: Bonhoeffer and the Practice of Nonviolence*, London: SPCK, 2004.

—— *The State of the University: Academic Knowledge and the Knowledge of God*, Oxford: Blackwell, 2007.

Hauerwas, Stanley, with Richard Bondi and David B. Burrell, *Truthfulness and Tragedy: Further Investigations into Christian Ethics*, 2nd edn, Notre Dame: University of Notre Dame Press, 1985.

Hauerwas, Stanley, and L. Gregory Jones (eds), *Why Narrative?*, Grand Rapids: Eerdmans, 1989.

Hauerwas, Stanley, and William H. Willimon, *Resident Aliens: Life in the Christian Colony*, Nashville: Abingdon Press, 1989.

Hauerwas, Stanley, and William H. Willimon, *Where Resident Aliens Live: Exercises for Christian Practices*, Nashville: Abingdon Press, 1996.

Hauerwas, Stanley, and Charles Pinches, *Christians Among the Virtues: Theological Conversations with Ancient and Modern Ethics*, Notre Dame: University of Notre Dame Press, 1997.

Hauerwas, Stanley, Chris K. Heubner, Harry J. Heubner and Mark Thiessen Nation, *The Wisdom of the Cross: Essays in Honor of John Howard Yoder*, Grand Rapids: Eerdmans, 1999.

Hauerwas, Stanley, and Samuel Wells (eds), *The Blackwell Companion to Christian Ethics*, Oxford: Blackwell, 2006.

Huntington, Samuel P., *The Clash of Civilizations and the Remaking of World Order*, London: Touchstone, 1998.

Hunsinger, George and William C. Placher (eds), *Theology and Narrative: Selected Essays*, Oxford: Oxford University Press, 1993.

Insole, Christopher J., 'The Truth Behind Practices: Wittgenstein, Robinson Crusoe and Ecclesiology', *Studies in Christian Ethics*, 20.3, 2007, pp. 364–82.

Jenkins, Timothy, *Religion in English Everyday Life: An Ethnographic Approach*, Oxford: Berghahn Books, 1999.

Kallenberg, Brad J., *Ethics as Grammar: Changing the Postmodern Subject*, Notre Dame: University of Notre Dame Press, 2001.

Lash, Nicholas, *Holiness and Silence: Reflections on the Question of God*, Aldershot: Ashgate, 2004.

Lindbeck, George A., *The Nature of Doctrine: Religion in a Postliberal Age*, Philadelphia: Westminster Press, 1984.

Loughlin, Gerald, *Telling God's Story: Bible, Church and Narrative Theology*, Cambridge: Cambridge University Press, 1996.

McFague, Sally, *Metaphorical Theology: Models of God in Religious Language*, London: SCM, 1982.

MacIntyre, Alasdair, *After Virtue*, London: Duckworth, 1985.

—— *Whose Justice, Whose Rationality?*, London: Duckworth, 1988.

Mackey, James P., *Power and Christian Ethics*, Cambridge: Cambridge University Press, 1994.

McGrath, Alister E. (ed.), *Encyclopedia of Modern Christian Thought*, Oxford: Blackwell, 1993.

Milbank, John, *Theology and Social Theory: Beyond Secular Reason*, Oxford: Blackwell, 1990.

—— *The Word Made Strange: Theology, Language, Culture*, Oxford: Blackwell, 1997.

—— *Being Reconciled: Ontology and Pardon*, London: Routledge, 2003.

—— *The Future of Love: Essays in Political Theology*, London: SCM, 2009.

Milbank, John, Catherine Pickstock and Graham Ward (eds), *Radical Orthodoxy: A New Theology*, London and New York: Routledge, 1999.

Moltmann, Jürgen, *The Coming of God: Christian Eschatology*, London: SCM, 1996.

Morris, Jeremy (ed.), *Faith and Freedom: Exploring Radical Orthodoxy*, London: Affirming Catholicism, 2003.

Nelson, Paul, *Narrative and Morality: A Theological Inquiry*, University Park and London: Pennsylvania State University Press, 1987.

O'Donovan, Oliver, *Resurrection and the Moral Order: An Outline for Evangelical Ethics*, 2nd edn, Leicester: Apollos, 1994.

—— *The Desire of Nations: Rediscovering the Roots of Political Theology*, Cambridge: Cambridge University Press, 1996.

—— *The Ways of Judgment*, Cambridge: Eerdmans, 2005.

Ogletree, Thomas W., *The Use of the Bible in Christian Ethics*, Philadelphia: Fortress Press, 1987.

Patterson, Susan, *Realist Christian Theology in a Postmodern Age*, Cambridge: Cambridge University Press, 1999.

Pecknold, C. C., *Transforming Postliberal Theology: George Lindbeck, Pragmatism and Scripture*, London: T. & T. Clark, 2005.

Percy, Martyn, and Stephen Lowe (eds), *The Character of Wisdom: Essays in Honour of Wesley Carr*, Aldershot: Ashgate, 2004.

Percy, Martyn, and Ian Markham (eds), *Why Liberal Churches Are Growing*, London: T. & .T. Clark, 2006.

Radcliffe, OP, Timothy, *Sing a New Song: The Christian Vocation*, Dublin: Dominican Publications, 1999.

Ramsey, Paul, *War and the Christian Conscience: How Shall Modern*

War be Conducted Justly?, 4th edn, Durham: Duke University Press, 1976.

Rasmusson, Arne, *The Church as Polis: From Political Theology to Theological Politics as Exemplified by Jürgen Moltmann and Stanley Hauerwas*, Notre Dame: University of Notre Dame Press, 1995.

Rowland, Christopher (ed.), *The Cambridge Companion to Liberation Theology*, Cambridge: Cambridge University Press, 1999.

Sacks, Jonathan, *The Politics of Hope*, London: Jonathan Cape, 1997.

—— *The Dignity of Difference: How to Avoid the Clash of Civilizations*, London: Continuum, 2002.

Schwartz, Barry, *The Paradox of Choice: Why More is Less*, New York: HarperCollins, 2004.

Shanks, Andrew, *God and Modernity: A New and Better Way to do Theology*, London: Routledge, 2000.

Stroup, George W., *The Promise of Narrative Theology*, London: SCM, 1981.

Stout, Jeffrey, *Democracy and Tradition*, Princeton: Princeton University Press, 2004.

Taylor, Charles, *A Secular Age*, Cambridge MA: Belknap Press, 2007.

Thiemann, Ronald F., *Revelation as Theology: The Gospel as Narrated Promise*, Notre Dame: University of Notre Dame Press, 1985.

Thiessen Nation, Mark, and Samuel Wells (eds), *Faithfulness and Fortitude: In Conversation with the Theological Ethics of Stanley Hauerwas*, Edinburgh: T. & T. Clark, 2000.

Thiselton, Anthony C., *The Two Horizons: New Testament Hermeneutics and Philosophical Descriptions with Special Reference to Heidegger, Bultmann, Gadamer and Wittgenstein*, Grand Rapids: Eerdmans, 1980.

—— *New Horizons in Hermeneutics: The Theory and Practice of Transforming Biblical Reading*, London: HarperCollins, 1992.

—— *Interpreting God and the Postmodern Self*, Edinburgh: T. & T. Clark, 1995.

Thomson, John B., *The Ecclesiology of Stanley Hauerwas*, Aldershot: Ashgate, 2003.

—— *Church on Edge? Practising Christian Ministry Today*, London: Darton, Longman & Todd, 2004.

—— *DOXA: A Discipleship Course*, London: Darton, Longman & Todd, 2007.

Tomlinson, Dave, *The Post Evangelical*, London: Triangle, 1996.

Webster, John, *Barth's Moral Theology: Human Action in Barth's Thought*, Edinburgh: T. & T. Clark, 1998.

Wells, Samuel, *Improvisation: The Drama of Christian Ethics*, London: SPCK, 2004.

Williams, Rowan, *Arius: Heresy and Tradition*, London: SCM, 2001.

—— 'The Body's Grace', Lesbian and Gay Christian Movement, 1989.

—— *Lost Icons: Reflections on Cultural Bereavement*, Edinburgh: T. & T. Clark, 2000.

—— *On Christian Theology*, Oxford: Blackwell, 2000.

—— *Anglican Identities*, London: Darton, Longman & Todd, 2004.

—— *Why Study the Past? The Quest for the Historical Church*, London: Darton, Longman & Todd, 2005.

Willimon, William H., and Stanley Hauerwas, with Scott C. Sage, *Lord Teach Us: The Lord's Prayer and the Christian Life*, Nashville: Abingdon Press, 1996.

Yoder, John H., *The Original Revolution: Essays in Christian Pacifism*, Scottdale: Herald Press, 1971.

—— *The Politics of Jesus*, 2nd edn, Grand Rapids: Eerdmans, 1982.

—— *The Priestly Kingdom: Social Ethics as Gospel*, Notre Dame: Notre Dame University Press, 1984.

Index